THE LITURGY AFTER VATICAN II

DENIS CROUAN, S.T.D.

THE
LITURGY AFTER
VATICAN II

Collapsing or Resurgent?

TRANSLATED BY MARK SEBANC

IGNATIUS PRESS   SAN FRANCISCO

Original French edition:
La Liturgie après Vatican II:
Effondrement ou redressement?
© 1999 Pierre Téqui, Paris

Cover design by Roxanne Mei Lum

ISBN 0–89870–841–9
Library of Congress control number 2001088859
Printed in the United States of America ⊗

When it comes to the liturgy, we should seek what is right and good rather than novelties that are apt to be pleasing only in the short term.

The author of this book is a French theologian, and he is describing the liturgical crisis in France. But while his examples are taken from that French context, his experience and the conclusions he draws are, as you will find, entirely applicable to the United States, Canada, and the United Kingdom. The Church is One and Catholic, and the liturgical malaise is not limited to our parishes or even our nation. We think that Dr. Crouan's analysis is both succinct and accurate. While it may be discouraging to realize how widespread in the Church the liturgical confusion is, it is encouraging to know that others, wholly independently, are responding vigorously, with "zeal for the Lord's house".

Joseph Fessio, S.J.
Editor, Ignatius Press

Contents

Preface

As can well be imagined, my book entitled *The Liturgy Betrayed*[1] attracted a certain amount of critical comment. Strangely enough, these critical sentiments were expressed by two groups of the faithful that are to all outward appearances antagonistic to one another. These are:

— the group consisting of those who reject the liturgy that was restored after Vatican II and who maintain with conviction that only the rites that were used before the Council remain true to a liturgical tradition that is authentically Catholic.

— the significant group that consists of those who, for the last thirty years, have falsified the liturgy of the Council in our parishes. These people claim that the celebrations presently occurring in almost all our churches are true to the teaching of the Constitution on the Sacred Liturgy, *Sacrosanctum concilium*, as well as the Roman Missal as restored after Vatican II.

Thus it is that brothers who are supposedly enemies find themselves on the same footing, since, in either case, they are pursuing a strategy whose end term, when all is said and done, is a rejection of the liturgy as defined by the Magisterium. Both groups think that they, instead of

---

[1] San Francisco: Ignatius Press, 2000.

the Church, are entitled to decide for themselves what form the "source and summit"[2] of the life of the Church should take. Therefore they refuse to take into account the teachings of the Holy See.

But *The Liturgy Betrayed* also resulted in my receiving letters of encouragement and gratitude. They came from numerous members of the faithful weary of having to participate every Sunday in "the wholesale liquidation of a rich patrimony of chants, formulas, and customs that neither the Council nor the reforms that came after the Council had ever required, but which has been deemed nevertheless to be part of the liturgical reform".[3]

I received mail from "rank-and-file faithful", as one might describe them, who confessed that, upon reading my study, they had come to understand they had been fooled, inasmuch as they had been led to believe for years that certain rites had become optional, that Vatican II had given priests permission to modify the liturgy at will, that everything had to be simplified to the utmost, that the participation of laymen in the liturgy had to take place amidst a flurry of comings and goings around the altar and microphones, that the old altars had to be abandoned in favor of mobile structures turned toward the congregation, that Gregorian chant had been abolished, and that the use of Latin could only be considered in the exceptional context of liturgical rites predating the Council, but certainly not in the context of the current liturgy.

---

[2] See Vatican II, *Constitution on the Sacred Liturgy*, *Sacrosanctum concilium* (December 4, 1963), no. 10 (hereafter abbreviated SC).

[3] Bishop Georges Lagrange, in *Enquête sur la messe traditionnelle*, *La Nef*, special issue no. 6 (1998).

The persons who wrote to me and whom I am anxious to thank here had discovered that all this was false: such a simplification and trivialization of the liturgy was never intended by Vatican II.

Finally I received the testimonies of priests—both young ones and not so young ones—who had been deprived of their ministry simply because, by refusing to modify the liturgy laid out by the current Roman Missal, they had put themselves at the margins of the current pastoral situation as it relates to the liturgy. This is a situation that has been arbitrarily imposed on them by colleagues occupying prominent positions in the diocesan bureaucracies.

Some of these priests have not hesitated to unburden themselves, venting their bitterness and deep suffering by posing a question that serves as an excellent summary of the current state of affairs: "The Pope issued the motu proprio *Ecclesia Dei* for those who are attached to the old Missal. Isn't it also high time that he issued an indult for all the priests who want to respect the current Missal but are prevented from doing so?"

For, curiously enough, in the climate of today's Church, the breakdown in the channels of authority that link the Head with the members is such that any diocesan priest who wanted to implement the teaching of the Magisterium—which should be considered just a bare minimum in the scheme of things—would in many cases need a dispensation from Rome to do so.

Lastly, there are countless people who have said to me, in virtually identical words: "Every Sunday, we find ourselves saddled with a Mass where the liturgy has been modified; we put up a fight for the liturgy of the Council, but all to no avail: the situation is only getting worse. . . . So, as things stand, we have ended up searching high and low for a Mass where the liturgy—it matters little whether it be the liturgy of Saint Pius V or that of Paul VI—is strictly respected."[4]

Do these personal testimonies not serve to show the great weariness of many of the faithful, as well as the enormous confusion—not to mention ignorance—that holds sway today in the area of the liturgy? Do they not prove that what is required by the majority of the faithful who have kept a real liking for the liturgy and are still practicing their faith is not so much celebrations that are "pastorally correct" as a eucharistic liturgy that offers all the guarantees of Catholicity and leads, by its stability and its beauty, to an authentic contemplation of the mysteries that are being celebrated?

In an era in which it has become commonplace to ask forgiveness, it has become urgent to clarify matters by having the courage to acknowledge the errors that have been made in the recent past. This is the only way the situation can be rectified in terms of establishing a greater fidelity to the real teaching of Vatican II and to the Roman Missal that is its fruit.

---

[4] During a conference that was held on May 2, 1998, by CIEL [Centre International d'Études Liturgiques], the participants assisted at a "present-day" liturgy that was impeccably celebrated at the Brompton Oratory. Michael Davies, who was the president of CIEL at the time, made the following remark in the course of his lecture: "If everyone had celebrated the Mass of Paul VI as they do at Brompton, there would not have been any problems." It should be noted that CIEL is committed to the old liturgy.

To this end, it is necessary first and foremost to examine what is being said and done these days in parish churches. Next, an effort must be made to note the possible errors, indeed snares, in which believers are apt to get themselves tangled even when they are in good faith. Often they have lost their essential points of reference, and because this is the case, they have no idea either whom they should believe or whom they should follow.

Our Roman liturgy bemoans its poverty. Has the time not come when those who have been appointed by the Church as the "overseers of the liturgy", in other words, the diocesan bishops, should have the courage to speak out loud and clear in order to put an end to what has become, in effect, a "debate over rites" that leaves everyone dissatisfied and betrayed?

CHAPTER ONE

What Is a Liturgical Rite?

What is a rite? This is the first question we must try to answer if we want to lay some of the groundwork that would afford us a better grasp of the reasoning developed in this study. A liturgical rite is a difficult thing to define. Nevertheless, it can be said that every rite normally constitutes a restrictive form of the official worship rendered to God. This form is comprised of elements that are harmoniously linked to one another and arise from the customs that are first accepted by a particular community and then approved by the legitimate ecclesiastical authority.

Let us examine this definition in further detail:

— Restrictive form of worship: the form of worship is normative for all the faithful, whatever their function in the Church. The Pope, bishops, pastors, deacons, the lay faithful: they all have to respect the form of worship.

— Comprised of elements harmoniously linked to one another: the different parts of the rite are not added to one another in an arbitrary, heterogeneous, or subjective fashion; they are arranged according to a logic

that is determined by a theology that offers every guarantee of being Catholic.

— Customs accepted by a community: a rite is not made
up of elements imposed by a person or by a group of
persons, but of usages that have progressively become
normative in and of themselves in a community whose
members were linked together by one and the same
Credo. Thus these usages have resulted in identifying
patterns of behavior.

— Approved by the ecclesiastical authority: it is a function of legitimate authority (the Holy See) to pronounce whether the implementation of any given rite
involves a risk either to the faith of each of the individuals who make up the community or to the co-
hesion of the community itself. It is a prerogative of
the authority to verify whether any given liturgical
practice brings with it the risk that it might lead to an
irregular spirituality.

Thus the legitimate authority can, without detriment
to the rite inasmuch as the authority is itself subject to
it, exercise the role of regulator. To the authority belongs the right to pronounce whether or not any given
element of a rite carries the risk of leading the believer
toward an ill-founded spirituality (in which case it would
be necessary to modify or abolish the element in question) and also whether or not any other given element in
a rite carries the risk of causing the believer to deviate
toward an overly subjective faith, a faith that is for this
reason detached from the common *Credo* (in which case

care would have to be taken to highlight the objective character of the rite).

What impact can a liturgical rite have on the believer? A liturgical rite is like the Ark of the Covenant that is spoken of in the Old Testament: Nobody can really say what it contains, for it is at once too mysterious and too rich to be confined by any reductive definition that our human capacity for words might ascribe to it.

If the Ark of the Covenant was the place where God made his presence known in the midst of his people, a liturgical rite is the means by which God renders himself really present. This presence is achieved through a liturgy whose meaning goes far beyond what the intellect can understand and far beyond what human words can formulate and transmit. In this regard, the liturgy ought to be fascinating: the power of fascination is one of the characteristics of all liturgy.

The liturgy, established around rites that constitute a framework, as it were, without which a true celebration would not be possible, suggests the Christian faith: it does not explain everything that man would like to understand and could possibly understand on a theological plane, but by its objectivity it confesses with exactitude the *Credo* of the Church. It displays the essentials of the faith to all the faithful, and to each member of the faithful in particular it points out the direction he ought to take in order to lead an authentic Christian life.

In this sense, it can be said that the liturgy is at once a source of graces and an authentic witness to the love of God. That is why the Church describes her liturgy with the qualifier "divine".

While the role of the liturgical rite is to enable a member of the faithful to live in the faith of the Church, it does not, however, have the power to proclaim the whole content of this faith. This is not its primary goal.

Why so? Because whereas the catechism addresses itself primarily to the intellect, in other words, to the consciousness of the person, the liturgy, for its part, should address itself essentially to the imagination. The imagination should be one of the liturgy's principal fields of action, for in the event of a conflict between the intellect and the imagination,[1] it is always the imagination that wins the day, inasmuch as it is the repository of our beliefs: what we imagine, what we believe, what appears true to us. What we imagine is more fundamental than what we do, for it is, in the final analysis, the motor force of our actions. It steers and directs us. It touches on a whole network of references, values, and beliefs and is responsible for our whole way of living and being.[2] These factors are an essential consideration for the person who wants to arrive at a proper understanding of how the system of liturgical rites functions. They help to explain in part how it was the liturgy alone that enabled faith to be kept in communist countries where atheism was mandatory for more than seventy years.

Since it is not the role of a rite to explain everything, there should be no offense taken if all the faithful do not comprehend the whole meaning of the liturgy. Immensely

---

[1] By "imagination" here we mean a structure that is constitutive of the conscious person and that is not to be confused with the imaginary.

[2] Cf. *Feu et lumière* 65 (September 1998): 12ff.

rich as it is, the liturgy occupies a place that is beyond our normal, everyday means of comprehension.

All the same, never should the mistake be made of arguing to the effect that, since the faithful do not understand all of it, the liturgy should be simplified for them or explained to them as it unfolds. The net result of this approach to the liturgy is not to make the rites more accessible, but rather to impoverish and disfigure them, to bring to naught the range of their symbolism and thus to destroy the liturgy itself.

Rather than explaining the liturgical rites at the very moment they are being performed, people need to learn to live them, so as to understand them in slow stages from within the celebration, in other words, with the eyes of faith and in relation to that which comprises the very heart of every liturgical celebration: the presence of the Lord on the altar.

This is the way that the liturgical rites can also become means of promoting sound social behavior and attitudes that are in keeping with the demands of the Christian life.

All of this is a good demonstration of the scope that the liturgy is capable of achieving: when all is said and done, if true rites that are correctly performed are effective means of inducing sound behavior, error-filled rites that are arbitrarily constructed always run the risk of becoming vehicles for false, ambiguous behavior or for poorly regulated religious devotions.

CHAPTER TWO

The Roman Rite before Vatican II

Fifteen years after the promulgation of the encyclical *Mediator Dei* by Pope Pius XII, John XXIII opened the Second Vatican Council.

It was on December 4, 1963, that the Council promulgated its first document. This was the constitution *Sacrosanctum concilium*, a text that deals with the liturgy and lays the groundwork for a "restoration" of the Roman Rite rather than a transformation of it.

What exactly did people mean when they referred to the Roman Rite at the time of the Council's opening? The Roman Rite is one of the liturgical forms used by the Church to celebrate the Lord: it makes use of prayers, hymns, symbols, gestures, and attitudes that, by the way they are formulated and organized, demonstrate the objective faith of the Church and allow it to be handed down. Like every liturgical rite, the Roman Rite finds its summit in the celebration of the Eucharist: the Mass. Throughout our study, therefore, it is the celebration of the Mass according to the Roman Rite that is going to be our point of focus.

Where does the "Roman Rite" come from? The main lines of it come from Rome, from the Roman Curia, to be exact. In other words, it stems from the Pope and his inner circle. In a way, the "Roman Rite" is heir to the way in which the first Christians in Rome celebrated.[1]

Nevertheless, this way they had of celebrating was not preserved undisturbed: in the course of the centuries, it was modified. In certain respects it was simplified (ancient customs fell into oblivion or lost their reason for being), while in other respects it underwent enlargement (certain historical circumstances or the influence of popular traditions may have led to a repetition or amplification of prayers or gestures that were considered expressive).

In the sixteenth century, on account of the vicissitudes that the Rite had undergone (modifications, simplifications, and developments), the Council of Trent decided on a first restoration of the Roman liturgy. This restoration was particularly needed at that time because the Rite had to be the vehicle for a sound body of doctrine that could be affirmed in the face of the theological currents arising from the Protestant Reformation.

Furthermore, at a time when there were multiple variations of the Roman liturgy in existence, stemming as they did from local customs, the restored Rite also had to be an instrument that allowed the unity of the Church to be made manifest: this is why the Roman Rite as revised and corrected at Trent ended up being observed everywhere and why it was to replace all the other ways of celebrating the Eucharist that could not lay claim to a tradition that was at least two hundred years old, in other words,

---

[1] Denis Crouan, *L'Histoire du Missel romain* (Paris: Téqui, 1988).

a tradition that went back to the end of the thirteenth century.[2]

It was Pope Saint Pius V who "respecified" the composition of the Roman rites according to strict criteria, leaving no room for improvisation. These respecified rites were given a detailed explanation in the first few pages of the Missal that was brought out in 1570.

In the preface to this Roman Missal published under his auspices, Pius V declared:

> We have decided and we ordain, under penalty of our wrath, that for all the other churches mentioned above,[3] the use of their own missals be discontinued and absolutely and totally abandoned and that nothing should be added, subtracted, or altered in the Missal that we have recently published. We have strictly decided for each and every one of the churches enumerated above, for the patriarchs, administrators, and all other persons vested with any ecclesiastical dignity, be they even Cardinals of the Holy Roman Church or possessed of any other rank or preeminence, that henceforth they should, by virtue of their holy obedience, abandon and totally reject all the other rules and rites, no matter how ancient, coming from other missals that they have been accustomed to using, and that they are to sing or say Mass according to the rite, manner, and norms herein laid down by us and that, in celebrating

---

[2] In other words, before the beginning of the decline of the Middle Ages.

[3] What he is talking about here are cathedrals, collegiate churches, churches belonging to a monastic order, whether of men or of women, parish churches, and chapels where the liturgy must be celebrated according to the Roman Rite.

Mass, it is not acceptable for them to add ceremonies or
recite prayers that are not in this Missal.[4]

But the celebration of the Eucharist in the Roman
Rite, as given by Saint Pius V, did not long withstand
the trials of history and of time: it was modified by Gre-
gory XIII and Sixtus V, who were the immediate successors of Pius V. Afterward it was revised and corrected
by Clement VIII, Urban VIII, Benedict XIV, and Leo
XIII. In more recent times, it became Saint Pius X's turn
to introduce substantial modifications to it. Finally, even
before the Council, in 1962, John XXIII made some additions to it.[5]

It was precisely this Roman Missal of 1962 that, at the
time of the Council, became the object of a restoration
whose basic framework was defined by the Vatican II
constitution *Sacrosanctum concilium*.

In February 1964, in order to put this restoration into
practice, Pope Paul VI created a Committee for the Implementation of the Constitution on the Sacred Liturgy,
which was chaired by Cardinal [Giacomo] Lercaro [1891–

---

[4] From the bull *Quo primum tempore*, dated July 14, 1570. In fact,
Saint Pius V's ban on adding or subtracting anything from the Missal
he had published under his auspices was not really obeyed. From the
eighteenth century onward into the nineteenth, local liturgies grew
in number, and in French dioceses in particular the bishops brought
out "their own" versions of the Roman Missal. It was Dom Guéranger
[Dom Prosper Guéranger, 1806–1875], the restorer of Benedictine life
to Solesmes, who was one of the first to launch a great campaign in
favor of liturgical unity and the restoration of the Roman Rite.

[5] Cf. the communication given by Dom Guy-Marie Oury, in *Actes
du colloque de Solesmes* (Rosheim: Association Pro Liturgia, 1999).

1976]. It did not take long for this committee (or Consilium) to issue practical directives. In September 1964 it pointed out that the use of vernacular languages was authorized [by the Council] in certain parts of the Mass in place of the Latin that had been in use up to that point.

Furthermore, the Consilium advised (even while asking pastors to exercise the utmost prudence and without making it obligatory) that it favored a celebration of the Mass "facing the people" wherever it could be done without harm to the architectural integrity of a church.[6]

In fact, it was from these authorizations granted by the Consilium that two great upheavals, which had in no way been foreseen or planned by the Second Vatican Council at its outset, took their rise: the abandonment of Latin as well as Gregorian chant, together with the widespread adoption of altars "facing the people", which were improperly positioned in front of older altars,[7] the latter being quickly abandoned by celebrants who were keen on anything that might give an aspect of newness to the way they celebrated Mass.

But, in very short order, the abandonment of Latin and Gregorian chant, coupled with the erection of secondary altars "facing the people", had other consequences. Let us cite two such consequences that are among the most

---

[6] Cf. Klaus Gamber, *Tournés vers le Seigneur* (Le Barroux: Sainte-Madeleine, 1993).

[7] Cf. *Notitiae*, cited in *Pro Liturgia*'s bulletin no. 82 (October 1995), and Bishop Tena in *Bulletin du secrétariat de la Conférence des évêques de France*, no. 5 (March 1995).

significant: an inordinate taste for improvisation and the abandonment of the notion of ceremony in the liturgy.

While the constitution *Sacrosanctum concilium* expressly asks priests to make no additions, changes, or subtractions to the liturgy on their own authority,[8] they became so used to altering the rituals that it did not take long for Masses to become personalized ceremonies in which the Roman Rite was no longer in evidence except as a pretext for adapting the liturgy to the whim of a celebrant or the pastoral demands of a situation.

The widespread adoption of changes and "adaptations" to the Roman Rite has led to the abandonment of liturgical ceremony: celebrations have been reduced to a minimal framework, the tendency of which has been to give the faithful a conception of the liturgy that is ever more impoverished and utterly devoid of eloquent expression.

As for Gregorian chant, it has been replaced by hymns (and it is generally acknowledged nowadays that most of them are worthless) and by simple refrains that are often incapable of edifying those of the faithful who are still going to church.[9] Thus it is the very notion of liturgy that is being lost.[10]

Therefore, between what the Second Vatican Council

---

[8] In fact, article 22 of the constitution on the liturgy reiterates the terms of *Quo primum tempore*, the bull of Saint Pius V.

[9] On this subject, see Paul VI's letter *Sacrificium laudis* (1966).

[10] Bishop Pablo Colino, choirmaster at St. Peter's in Rome, "Les Notes perdues et la confusion du peuple", *30 Jours* 2 (1998); Maurice Tillie, "Le Chant grégorien au coeur du renouveau liturgique", in *Bulletin Pro Liturgia* 115 (1998).

calls for and what has been imposed on the faithful there is a gulf that has gotten wider and wider.

It has not taken long for reactions to set in: Pierre Debray has established the movement known as Les Silencieux de l'Église [the Church's Silent Members], which held one of its first meetings at Strasbourg; Bernadette Lecureux has brought out *Le Latin, langue de l'Église* [Latin, the language of the Church],[11] a brilliant work that raises some essential and critical questions; also, in Paris, Georges Cerbelaud-Salagnac has established the Una Voce Association, whose goal is to safeguard and develop the Latin liturgy, Gregorian chant, and sacred art within the Roman Catholic Church.[12]

Besides these moderate movements, which, at the outset at least, did not question the Council itself so much as the slanted interpretations that have been made of it, as well as the erroneous implementations that these interpretations have given rise to, there have been other movements that take matters farther, for their demand pure and simple is that the constitution *Sacrosanctum concilium* be scrapped and that the liturgy defined by the Roman Missal in use up until 1962 be preserved and retained.

---

[11] A new edition of this work was published in 1997 by Téqui with a preface by Dom Philippe Dupont, Abbot of Saint-Pierre de Solesmes.

[12] At its inception, it was the goal of the Una Voce Association to safeguard and develop the Latin liturgy, Gregorian chant, and sacred art within the Roman Catholic Church. Nowadays, however, it seems that the goal of the association is to safeguard and develop the Latin liturgy and Gregorian chant within the framework of the Missal of 1962, even while casting aspersions at times on the celebration of the Roman liturgy according to the dictates of Vatican II.

It is this last point that is insisted upon by those of the faithful who follow Archbishop Lefebvre.

From this situation, three main tendencies have become clear in a liturgical context that bears more and more resemblance to a potluck dinner where the only dish a person is apt to find is what he himself has brought with him for the occasion:

— the *traditionalist* tendency, which demands the preservation of the preconciliar Roman Rite, such as it was defined in the main by Saint Pius V, and which blames Vatican II for being the source of the most pressing evils that have plagued the postconciliar Church.

— the genuinely *conciliar* tendency, which for over thirty years has demanded (although by and large in vain) a correct implementation of Vatican II and wants the liturgy to be celebrated according to the norms of the authorized Roman Missal.

— the *so-called conciliar* tendency, which holds sway in most parishes and which imposes as many variations on the Roman liturgy as there are celebrants, each of these variations constituting a fresh new betrayal, in its own fashion, of Vatican II.

CHAPTER THREE

One Roman Rite or
Several Roman Rites?

Anxious to put an end to what is commonly called "the debate over rites", certain traditionalist or conservative circles demand that two rites of the Mass should be allowed to coexist: the so-called Rite of Saint Pius V and the so-called Rite of Paul VI.[1]

In other circles, what is envisioned is a "fusion of these two rites". It is thought that this would please a majority of today's dissatisfied faithful and put an end to the liturgical abuses that have grown in number after Vatican II and that exist in numerous places.[2]

What should we think of these two solutions that have been proposed with a view to solving the current problems regarding the liturgy? To answer this question, we must start by studying the current state of the liturgy more closely.

It is obvious that for a coexistence or a fusion of rites

---

[1] A position championed today by associations such as Una Voce, CIEL, La Nef, etc.

[2] Cf. *Enquête sur la messe traditionnelle*, a study published in 1998 by *La Nef* (special issue no. 6) on the occasion of the tenth anniversary of the motu proprio *Ecclesia Dei adflicta*.

to be considered possible, there would have to be at least two distinct liturgical rites recognized by the Church.

From this there arises a preliminary question: Is it true that two Roman Rites of the Mass exist, that of Saint Pius V, on the one hand, which was in use up until the Second Vatican Council, and, on the other hand, the Rite of Paul VI, which took its rise in the wake of Vatican II, its aim being to replace that of Saint Pius V? A quick historical survey allows us to answer this question.

What liturgies could be found in the Catholic Church up until the time of the Council? The simplest answer that can be given is the following: the Catholic Church encompassed two great liturgical families, the one Eastern and the other Western.

In the Eastern family, for example, there could be found the Maronite Rite (in Lebanon), the Coptic Rite (in Egypt), the Rite of Saint John Chrysostom (in different areas of Eastern Europe), and so on.

In the Western family, for example, there could be found the Hispanic Rite (in Spain), the Ambrosian Rite (in Milan), the Lyonnese Rite (in Lyons), the Cistercian Rite (in Cistercian monasteries), the Dominican Rite (in Dominican houses), and, in the main, the Roman Rite, more or less the direct heir to the papal liturgy used in Rome in days of old.

For historical reasons, the Roman Rite had become the most common, the most universal, and the best known: it was the most widely used rite for the celebration of the eucharistic liturgy throughout the world.

Thus, in the area of Europe where we live, there was every chance that the faithful who went to a parish church to participate in the Mass were able to participate in a liturgy celebrated according to the Roman Rite.

As this Rite was very precisely codified and closely linked to the use of the Latin language, the faithful were assured of finding the same prayers, the same singing (basically Gregorian chant), the same signs, and the same gestures everywhere. Thus everybody's participation was greatly facilitated, with the help of a Mass book that gave useful translations and explanations.

Before the Council, the book that priests used for the celebration of Mass and that laid out in detail the arrangement of the Roman Rite bore as its title: *Missale romanum* (Roman Missal). It would never have dawned on anybody to call this Roman Missal the Missal of Saint Pius V or the Traditional Missal. This would have seemed utterly absurd. Up until the time of the Council you would never have heard anyone refer to the Missal of Saint Pius V. It would never have dawned on anybody to suppose or teach that one fine day Pope Pius V had concocted a Missal that would bear his name.

In fact, it must be reiterated here that a Pope can no more "concoct" a Missal than he can devise a liturgical rite on his own authority and initiative. Only the living tradition of the Church can give birth to rites. The Popes can only check to see if the development of these rites includes anything contradictory to the faith of the Church and whether there is any risk that they might lead to badly regulated patterns of behavior among the faithful. After that, the Popes submit to liturgical rites, as for that matter must all the faithful submit to them, whether they be clergy or laymen. So here we have the first element of an answer to the question that was posed above: There was no such thing as a Rite of Saint Pius V either before or during the Second Vatican Council.

With all the more reason, there is no such thing as a Rite of Saint Pius V after the Council. To claim the opposite, as do many traditionalist movements which take advantage of the vagueness and uncertainty of the current situation, comes under the heading of historical and theological error, and, what is more serious, it betrays a willingness to feed false information to the faithful.

CHAPTER FOUR

The Line of Argument
Pursued by the Traditionalists

As a general rule, the various traditionalist groups teach that, in the wake of Vatican II, committees of experts acting in concert with numerous bureaucracies created a completely new rite that had hardly any connection at all with the Roman Rite that had been the object of participation on the part of the faithful up until the time of the Council.

Thus traditionalists maintain that Vatican II marked a break with long-held liturgical tradition and for this reason engendered two Roman Rites: the old Rite, which, according to them, is the only witness to the authentic tradition, and the new Rite, developed by theologians who were more or less affected by the progressivism that held sway at the time of the Council.[1]

Since these same traditionalists reckon that what they call the new Rite no longer has any connection with the authentic Roman liturgical tradition, they attach great importance to keeping alive the old form of the Roman Rite (which they wrongly call the Rite of Saint Pius V or also

---

[1] "The new *ordo* was concocted artificially", in Pierre Debray's *Courrier Hebdomadaire*, 1322 (July 1998).

the classic Roman Rite) and call for its preservation as well as the new liturgy, which some of them go so far as to reject, describing it as heretical, even though it has been acknowledged by the Supreme Pontiffs who succeeded Paul VI: John Paul I and John Paul II.

To justify the preservation of two parallel ritual forms, as it were, traditionalist movements base themselves primarily on article 4 of the constitution *Sacrosanctum concilium*, which states that the Council recognizes the equality of all the rites in terms of both their authority and their dignity.

Then, in order to have this article 4 serve the cause they have militantly taken up, these same traditionalists decree on their own authority that the preconciliar form of the Roman liturgy should be regarded as an autonomous rite, distinct from the liturgy created after the Council.

What we have here is a hasty conclusion that is the result of an erroneous reading of the text of the Council in general and of article 4 of the constitution *Sacrosanctum concilium* in particular. In fact, such an interpretation of article 4 introduces the notion that a rite was created, and nothing, either in the texts of the Council or even in the teachings of the Popes, allows such a view to be justified or indeed proposed.

But there is a sleight of hand being practiced here. When we look at the traditionalist movements that often claim to be the most moderate, all they have to do to prove their moderation is ask for the coexistence of the two so-called rites: the preconciliar rite and the postconciliar rite. According to them, this would be a way of putting an end to the debate over rites.

Finally, to show that such a coexistence would be in full conformity with the great liturgical tradition of the Church, traditionalist faithful base their argument on the fact that in the East no less than in the West there has always been a great diversity of rites and that this diversity has been a source of enrichment.[2]

Here again, the error must be denounced: Both in the East and in the West the different rites recognized by the Church are autonomous rites that were born in sociohistorical contexts that are distinct from one another and that developed in uninterrupted traditions all related to a common liturgical source. Thus these different rites, all recognized by the Magisterium, did not stem from the rejection or acceptance of an older ritual form, as would be the case with regard to the Roman Rite if one wanted to uphold the arguments made by traditionalist groups.

So if a person felt bound to subscribe to the theory held by traditionalist movements, he would have to concede that only the faithful attached to the preconciliar Roman liturgy are Roman Rite Catholics; as for the rest of the faithful, having accepted the Council's Constitution on the Sacred Liturgy, they would be something like Vatican or Neo-Roman Rite Catholics.

Now, as we have seen, in the eyes of the Church there is no such thing as a Vatican Rite or a Neo-Roman Rite. The Church recognizes only one Roman Rite, and the verbal gymnastics that traditionalist groups have recourse

---

[2] See, for example, the study of Don Pietro Cantoni, "Pour une juste interprétation du motu proprio *Ecclesia Dei*", in *Enquête sur la messe traditionnelle*, special issue no. 6 of *La Nef*, 1998.

to, in their efforts to give special designations to certain phases of this selfsame Roman Rite, do not correspond to any reality.

In the final analysis, what is necessary is a proper interpretation of article 4 of the Council's Constitution on the Sacred Liturgy, which affirms the equality in terms of both authority and dignity of all the rites legitimately recognized by the Church.

Article 4 teaches without the slightest bit of ambiguity that in tackling the revision of the one sole Roman Rite, the Council did not want to lead people to believe that the other rites recognized by the Church (the Eastern rites and the Western rites apart from the Roman Rite) would have a lesser value in the eyes of the Magisterium.

Vatican II teaches that all liturgies apart from the Roman, whether they be Eastern or Western, have the same value as the Roman liturgy, to which the Fathers of the Council found they had to turn their attention, in order to restore it and give it back its first splendor. This teaching is important insofar as it recalls the identical value of the Western and Eastern sources of our liturgy.[3]

In no way does Article 4 mean that the Council intended to create a new rite which would give the Roman liturgy in use until the time of Vatican II, whose arrangement is defined by the Missal of 1962, the right to be considered an autonomous rite (a so-called Rite of Saint Pius V or Tridentine Rite) whose equality in terms

---

[3] John Paul II, the apostolic letter *Orientale lumen* (May 2, 1995); Bishop Bernard Dupire, in *Actes du Colloque de Solesmes* (Rosheim: Association Pro Liturgia, 1999).

of authority and dignity would have to be recognized in tandem with the new rite. The critical mistake made by almost all the traditionalist movements is to be found in their faulty reading and erroneous interpretation of Article 4 of the constitution *Sacrosanctum concilium*.

CHAPTER FIVE

What the Council Really Wanted

Did the Second Vatican Council really create a new liturgy, as is claimed today by numerous groups of the faithful who have been influenced by traditionalist movements?

Not by any means. The text of the constitution *Sacrosanctum concilium* states quite clearly that as its main objective the Council set itself the task of revising the ritual of the Roman Mass in order to facilitate the participation of the faithful in the liturgy. This was the agenda of the Council's Constitution on the Sacred Liturgy: no more and no less.

It is obvious that revising the ritual of the Roman Mass does not mean creating a new liturgy. For the Council Fathers it was a matter of faithfully retaining the substance of the rites of the Roman liturgy that had been preserved up to the time of Vatican II, even as they abolished secondary rites that had been added belatedly to the liturgy and that were often redundant. Possibly the plan was to reintroduce ancient rites that were part of the eucharistic celebration, traces of which could be found in the Missal of 1962, but which had been forgotten with time or progressively neglected.

The conclusion is self-evident: The Council did not create *ex nihilo* a new rite different from the Roman Rite in use up to the time of Vatican II. Both before and after the Council it has always been a matter of one and the same Roman Rite, even though it appears under two somewhat different aspects; in actual fact, these aspects are merely two more pronounced reflections of numerous phases that the development of the Roman liturgy has gone through in the course of the centuries.

If one wants to avoid spreading false notions, this is a point that must be insisted upon: Contrary to what is claimed by groups and movements that belong to the traditionalist sphere of influence, there is no substantial difference between the Roman liturgy before Vatican II and the Roman liturgy after Vatican II. Objectively, it can only be said that the Roman Missal that was in use before the Council and the one that is being used now after the Council set out precisely the same Roman Rite under two different but traditional aspects of its historical evolution.

That in the wake of the restored Roman Missal there have been deviations and acts of disobedience that are much more serious than the faithful have been led to believe, that there has been a certain anarchy and a process of desacralization that we all deplore, is another problem altogether. This problem is linked to the disobedience of clergy who have taken advantage of the silence and weakness of ecclesiastical authorities on the diocesan and national levels, but it is certainly not linked to the Council itself.

Incidentally, it must be asked whether the liturgical

restoration desired by Vatican II has not simply served to reveal a crisis that was latent before the Council. It is in fact quite interesting to note that priests who turned out to be the greatest destroyers of the liturgy *after* the Council are often those who were the most conservative in terms of the liturgy *before* the Council. Why this sudden about-face and this sudden desire to demolish the liturgy?

In the opinion of certain members of the clergy who were becoming more and more attracted to a social, humanistic approach, was not the preconciliar liturgy already a hollow sort of affair, like an envelope emptied of its spiritual content?

Psychologists would not be ill-advised to turn their attention to this question; the answers that they would eventually be able to give might clarify the problematic crisis in the priesthood that the postconciliar Church has undergone.[1]

---

[1] Paul Vigneron, *Histoire des crises du clergé français contemporain* (Paris: Téqui, 1976).

CHAPTER SIX

Ecclesia Dei Adflicta

On June 30, 1988, Archbishop Marcel Lefebvre, regarded
as the leader of those Catholics attached to the liturgy as
it was before Vatican II, engaged in a schismatic act: he
consecrated several bishops without receiving permission
to do so from the Pope.

On July 2, in the wake of Archbishop Lefebvre's action,
which did grave harm to the unity of the Church, John
Paul II put out a motu proprio whose opening words in
Latin were: *Ecclesia Dei adflicta* ("With great sadness the
Church has learned of the unlawful episcopal ordination
conferred").[1]

In this motu proprio, the Pope asked that the spiritual desires of all those who feel bound to the Latin
liturgical tradition be respected everywhere, and he put
a broad and generous construction on the implementation of the directives given earlier (that is, on October 3,
1984) concerning the use of the Roman Missal of 1962.
Thus the Pope granted permission to those of the faithful
who, for various reasons, might be tempted to follow the
liturgical orientations of Archbishop Lefebvre to use precisely the same Missal as the one that Archbishop Lefeb-

---

[1] Cf. *Documentation catholique* 1967 (August 1988).

vre employed to celebrate Mass, which is to say, the Roman Missal in use before the Council. Thus the faithful
who were attached to the old liturgy could remain in the
Church without having to follow Archbishop Lefebvre in
his theological, pastoral, ideological, or political choices.

Nevertheless, there are two points that appear in the
very text of the motu proprio that need careful consideration, points about which there has been a general incli-
nation to keep silent:

First point: The Pope speaks about the Roman Missal
of 1962 and not about the Traditional Rite or the Rite
of Saint Pius V, as traditionalists generally do. Thus the
Sovereign Pontiff points out clearly that the way in which
the Mass was celebrated before Vatican II by no means
constitutes a separate rite that could as such coexist on a
long-term basis with the present-day liturgy, but simply
an earlier phase of the Roman liturgy.

Second point: If there is a genuine desire to understand the Pope's thinking, time has to be made to read
and study the whole text of the motu proprio and not just
a select paragraph here and there, where the temptation
would be to read into the text only what is favorable to
the cause that one intends to espouse. Thus, addressing
himself clearly to all the faithful and not just to the traditionalists, as is generally supposed, John Paul II writes:

> Indeed, the extent and depth of the teaching of the Sec-
> ond Vatican Council call for a renewed commitment to
> a deeper study in order to reveal clearly the Council's
> continuity with tradition, especially in points of doctrine
> which, perhaps because they are new, have not yet been
> well understood by some sections of the Church.

This passage is important for two reasons.

First of all, because the Sovereign Pontiff teaches clearly that, contrary to what is asserted by some groups that lay claim to the old form of the Roman liturgy, the form that stems from the Council, as described in the authorized edition of the Roman Missal, is totally connected to tradition. Therefore, in no way could a person—except in contradiction to the teaching of the Magisterium—present Vatican II as a council that breaks with the past or introduces a novelty.

Secondly, it is important because the Pope states that "some sections of the Church" do not have a proper understanding of the scope of Vatican II. Now at no time does the Pope give the impression here that these particular sections of the Church are comprised only of traditionalist faithful. In fact, here John Paul is addressing not only traditionalists who reject the fruits of the Council before they have tasted them, but all the progressives who for years have circulated false interpretations of the constitution *Sacrosanctum concilium* and have caused erroneous ways of using the present Roman Missal to become widespread and, by so doing, have precipitated the reaction of conservative groups and their attachment to the old liturgy.

This is why John Paul II, even in the same motu proprio, asks bishops to exercise clear-sighted vigilance in rejecting all erroneous interpretations and arbitrary, improper implementations in matters of doctrine, liturgy, and discipline. The analysis of the situation made by the Pope by way of his motu proprio shows clearly that the fact that some of the faithful have fallen back on the old form of the Roman liturgy is not attributable to the Council itself[2] but to the lack of discipline of those people— and unfortunately there are all too many of them—who have falsified the new form of the Roman liturgy.[3]

So first of all the motu proprio *Ecclesia Dei adflicta* has a purely pastoral scope: it aims at allowing so-called traditionalist faithful to remain in full communion with the entire Church through the old form of the liturgy, even as the Church awaits the day when the current liturgy is respected everywhere and thus is less offensive to the faithful as a whole.

But in no way can this motu proprio be construed as an act legitimizing the use of the form of the Roman Rite that was in use before the Council.[4] John Paul II makes this clear again in his apostolic letter *Vicesimus quintus an-*

---

[2] "I can tell you that for many years I have assisted at an impeccable celebration of the new *Ordo Missae* at the Brompton Oratory, my parish in London, and to repeat a comment made by Michael Davies himself on May 2 of this year at Wigmore Hall in London during a lecture to the CIEL, 'If everyone had celebrated the Mass of Paul VI as they do at Brompton, there would not have been any problems.' I am also thinking of places like . . . Solesmes, Saint-Wandrille, Kergonan or even St. Peter's in Rome, . . . where the celebration of the new Mass does not produce the same overall impression as it does in so many of our French parishes" (Letter of September 15, 1998, from a monk of Le Barroux on behalf of Abbot Gérard Calvet addressed to Denis Crouan, president of the Pro Liturgia Association).

[3] There are a few books that report on some of the difficulties that are encountered when it comes to the liturgy: Huguette Pérol, *Les Sans-papiers de l'Église* (Paris: F. X. de Guibert, 1996); Patrick Chalmel, *Ecône ou Rome: Le Choix de Pierre* (Paris: Fayard, 1990); Jacques de Ricomont, *Visites à Messieurs les Curés de Paris* (Paris: Table Ronde, 1981); André Frossard, *Le Parti de Dieu* (Paris: Fayard, 1992).

[4] Which is nonetheless what the Una Voce Association continues

nus, written on the occasion of the twenty-fifth anniversary [December 4, 1988] of the Council's Constitution on the Sacred Liturgy:

> The reform of the rites and the liturgical books was undertaken immediately after the promulgation of the constitution *Sacrosanctum concilium* and was brought to an effective conclusion in a few years thanks to the considerable and selfless work of a large number of experts and bishops from all parts of the world (cf. SC 25).
>
> This work was undertaken in accordance with the conciliar principles of fidelity to tradition and openness to legitimate development, and so it is possible to say that the reform of the liturgy is strictly traditional and in accordance with the ancient usage of the Holy Fathers (cf. SC 50).[5]

In the brief passage given here, let us point out several elements that need to be considered:

— The Pope speaks clearly about a reform of the rites of the Roman liturgy, not the creation of a new rite.

— The word "tradition" appears two times here to describe the current form of the liturgy; so it is impossible to claim that the motu proprio *Ecclesia Dei* should be perpetuated to allow the legitimization of the old Roman Rite. If such were the case, the old Roman Rite could be falsely construed as the only one in keeping with liturgical tradition.

---

to maintain (cf. editorial of no. 201 [July-August 1998]) at the risk of thus misleading some of the faithful.

[5] Apostolic letter *Vicesimus quintus annus* (December 4, 1988), no. 4.

— The formulaic phrase *ad normam Sanctorum Patrum*, "in accordance with the ancient usage of the Holy Fathers", is taken from the bull *Quo primum*,[6] by which Pope Saint Pius V, in the sixteenth century, showed that the work carried out under his authority to correct the Roman Missal had its roots in the liturgical tradition that had been kept alive by the Church.

This being the case, every member of the faithful must understand how absurd it is to demand the use of the old liturgical form on the grounds that it is more traditional than the current form, which the Church already regards as strictly traditional. Such an approach may perhaps have something to do with an emotional attachment to the old ceremonies, but certainly not with a keen sense of the liturgy and an objective vision of it.

In an interview, Patrick Le Gal, the bishop of Tulle, summarizes the question of the motu proprio issued by John Paul II in these terms:

> Proper use of the motu proprio does not lie in seeing it as a Godsend in terms of which permission to do something is finally granted, or as an option that is given to our freedom in its yearning to assert itself. Rather, the proper use of this document lies in our constantly consulting the truth and listening to the official word of the Church in order to learn anew how to tread the liberating path of obedience, especially with regard to liturgical life: of course, the first stage in this process is to follow the rules that are prescribed, and then to acquire a true un-

---

[6] See note 4 of chapter 2.

derstanding of their deeper import, and then to go farther
so as even to be able at times to renounce an option that
is merely permitted in order to prefer, out of regard for
the common good, a course of action that may be likened
to a high and excellent road.[7]

"To be able at times to renounce an option that is
merely permitted": is this not the high and excellent road
that should be followed not only by the traditionalists
who are prepared at all costs to make use of a mere permission given by the motu proprio *Ecclesia Dei adflicta*,
but also by most of the clergy and laity, who have little
training by and large when it comes to theology, but who
take advantage of all the allowances and all the exceptions
and by so doing no longer show any respect at all for the
liturgical norms?

Should the norm given by the Church for the celebration of the liturgy in the customary context of our parish
churches suddenly have less value than all the permissions
and dispensations given on ephemeral pastoral grounds,
whose validity in many cases is open to dispute? What
impact and what future will the Roman liturgy have if
it is constantly being celebrated without any heed being
paid to norms, in other words, if the celebrants themselves manufacture exceptional situations in an artificial
way in order to systematize arbitrary adaptations of the
eucharistic rite?

It is in the light of this question that we should under-

---

[7] In *Enquête sur la messe traditionnelle*, special issue no. 6 of *La Nef*,
(1998).

stand the point of view given by Bishop Ré, substitute in
the Vatican's Secretariat of State, to Mr. de Saventhem,
president of the International Una Voce Federation:

> The general law remains the use of the rite that has been
> renewed since the Council, whereas the use of the earlier
> rite falls at the moment under the heading of privileges
> that ought to keep the character of exceptions.[8]

Nevertheless, it is perfectly understandable how, in
the oftentimes anarchic liturgical situation that we are
presently experiencing, some of the faithful can be attached to the old form of the liturgy: in the final analysis,
it is the only means they have at their disposal to maintain
beauty and dignity in their celebrations and likewise to
preserve the use of Latin and Gregorian chant, whereas in
numerous places where people lay claim to the sanction
of the Council, these elements, which are essential to a
more complete expression of worship, have been abandoned or sometimes even totally banned.

On the other hand, it is less easy to understand how
some of the faithful can continue to request a coexistence
or a fusion of two rites, inasmuch as there is no such thing
as two Roman Rites, as we have seen. In actual fact, if
the Church wanted to concede the existence of two Roman Rites (a preconciliar one and a postconciliar one),
she would first have to acknowledge that the liturgy restored in the wake of Vatican II has no connection with
the traditional patrimony of the authentic Roman liturgy.
After which, the Magisterium would have to reformulate
completely the Council's Constitution on the Sacred Lit-

---

[8] Ibid.

urgy. In other words, when you come down to it, the essence of what *Sacrosanctum concilium* teaches would be put in question. A process like this would necessarily lead to declaring the constitutions of the Council optional.

As can be easily understood, such a position would open the door to a state of unspeakable liturgical anarchy in the Church. But is this perhaps what the progressive movements basically want, for they know full well how to use traditionalist movements as unwitting dupes by appearing at times to be quite tolerant toward their demands?

CHAPTER SEVEN

The Strategy of
Traditionalist Movements

The different movements attached to the liturgical forms
in use before Vatican II have a strategy that aims to win
over new followers for the preconciliar liturgy. This strategy works a little bit like a two-stage rocket.

First stage of the rocket: A person begins by practicing the
Coué Method[1] in order to convince himself that the form
of the Roman liturgy defined overall by Saint Pius V and
described by the rubrics of the Missal in use until 1962
constitutes a separate rite in itself, a rite that should be
recognized and upheld by the Church for the very reasons
given by the teaching contained in article 4 of the Constitution on the Sacred Liturgy. As we have seen above, this
is an erroneous interpretation of the texts of Vatican II.

Second stage of the rocket: Having obtained these results
through the Coué method, the traditionalists then seek
to gather together as many of the faithful as they can in
their churches and chapels. For this, they lean on a new ar-

---

[1] Emile Coué (1857–1926) was a French pharmacist who developed
a method of psychotherapy marked by the frequent, autosuggestive repetition of the formula, "Every day and in every way I am becoming
better and better."—TRANS.

gument, that of respect for various liturgical sensibilities, making reference to the declarations of such and such a theologian or such and such a prelate who is favorable to the old form of the liturgy.

It is obvious that theologians or prelates are totally free to have their opinions on liturgical questions; it should, however, be pointed out to the faithful that these opinions remain working hypotheses, which, as such, cannot be substituted for the teachings of the Magisterium.[2]

Would it not be appropriate, in the future, to see to it that the texts and documents coming from the Holy See be better propagated, in order to reduce the temptation of the faithful to refer only to what such and such a prelate, professor, or—worse still—journalist thinks about religious questions in general and liturgical questions in particular?

The current context lends itself to the implementation of such a strategy on the part of the traditionalist groups, inasmuch as the faithful, plunged for years into a kind of liturgical no-man's land, have lost sight of all their landmarks when it comes to the liturgy and imagine that what they see being done in the churches—things that are not

---

[2] The most harmful error in the current context of confusion would be to continue to believe or lead people to believe that the liturgy can be considered a question of sensibilities. The liturgy is first and foremost a question of truth and objectivity; although the implementation of the liturgy can effectively touch the sensibilities of the faithful at different levels of intensity and for different reasons, even so, one cannot set up a liturgical rite or establish a liturgical practice that fancies itself to be in keeping with the Church on the basis of the sensibilities espoused by one group or another. It is the liturgy which is the "source" and not the believer: it is the liturgy that makes the believer, not the opposite.

to their liking—is always in accordance with what the Council requested.

And since these members of the faithful no longer find it possible to participate in a Roman liturgy celebrated in exact accordance with the official books published in the wake of Vatican II, they fall back in good faith on the old liturgy, the only one that may currently be celebrated with a genuine respect for a Roman Missal.

But is this withdrawal into an old liturgical form, recognized by the Church in exceptional cases, a solution for the future? Do we not run the risk of witnessing the rise of all sorts of ghetto-chapels here, there, and everywhere, catering to ever more marginalized members of the faithful, who are destined to be reduced in the end to a psychological state in which they cling desperately to their certitudes and suspect that all the Church favors any more is doctrinal liberalism, which, of course, could never be the case?

The progressives, who everywhere favor anarchic liturgical forms and an evolutionary worship turned more toward man than toward God, have encouraged the faithful to give vent to their suffering by deserting the churches. But is this all the faithful deserve? Do they really deserve to be forced to flee so as to take refuge in groups that were formed solely because the errors that had filtered into the methods by which Vatican II was implemented had never been combatted effectively in the Church in France?

For all these reasons, we must avoid having the motu proprio *Ecclesia Dei adflicta* become an occasion for withdrawal into the old form of the Roman liturgy: this permission granted by John Paul II can only be a "springboard for the conversion and edification of the whole community"[3] around the liturgy celebrated as the Church demands and not around liturgies celebrated arbitrarily in churches "where the celebrant or the liturgical team are the reigning gurus".[4]

The strategy used by traditionalist groups is dangerous in that it prompts the faithful to band together in parallel chapels and conventicles but does not encourage them to discover the real liturgy given by the Church for the fostering and promotion of genuine spiritual growth.

---

[3] Bishop Patrick Le Gal, in *Enquête sur la messe traditionnelle*, special issue no. 6 of *La Nef*, (1998).

[4] Fr. Alain Bandelier, in *Famille chrétienne* 1071 (July 23, 1998).

CHAPTER EIGHT

Progressives: Beguiled by the Ambiguous Charms of the Liturgy

In almost all our parishes there can be found people responsible for the liturgy—priests and laity—who still think that the reason why eucharistic celebrations seem boring to many of the faithful is because they are governed by fixed rituals and precise rubrics: according to them, anything that is repeated every Sunday must by definition be wearisome.

This being the case, in order to make Sunday celebrations more attractive, these people in positions of responsibility imagine that they have to be constantly modifying the liturgy, constantly innovating, and, in order to do this, they no longer hesitate to distance themselves more or less from the official rites defined by the Church. Indeed, in the seventies and eighties, they went so far as to encourage "liturgical creativity" in parishes and seminaries, claiming that the Roman Missal should be no more than an aid for priests who were lacking in creative imagination.[1]

---

[1] See C. Wackenheim, a professor of fundamental theology, in *Entre la routine et la magie: La Messe* (Paris: Centurion, 1982), or also Cer-

This is why, in defiance of the teaching of the Church, they have gone so far as to teach that the celebrant should be free to adapt the form taken by his celebrations to the congregation that comes to his parish Masses.[2] This practice, which they have tried their hardest to make prevalent, justifying it by drawing on pastoral arguments (which many priests sincerely believe in), prompts us to ask two questions today:

— Can a person break free of the liturgical rites established by the Church without risk to the faithful?

— What particular role is played by the ritualization of the liturgy?

Can a person break free of the rites established by the Church without risk to the faithful?

1. How liturgical choices are made

The operation whereby the liturgy is modified by removing things from it or adding things to it, or by toning down or amplifying a rite or prayer, always presupposes the making of choices: a person has to choose to say this rather than that, to do things like this rather than like that, to suppress a given rite in order to replace it with some

---

cle Jean XXIII de Nantes, *Liturgie et lutte des classes* (Paris: Harmattan, 1976).

[2] This is what is still taught in numerous journals of pastoral liturgy that have enjoyed real success, especially with the "teams" entrusted with "liturgical animation" in our parishes.

other gesture that is thought to be more "meaningful",
and so on.

Now when you take a closer look at how these choices
are made, you notice that in most cases they are predi-
cated on a simple catch phrase: "It has to be appealing
and *more meaningful* for the faithful." In fact, however, the
person who chooses to adapt the liturgy to what he thinks
is the taste of the faithful is blindly following—in other
words, without the least claim to any measure of critical thought—information relayed in certain journals of
pastoral liturgy that recount experiments that have, they
firmly maintain, borne fruit and been a success.[3]

So the celebrant is invited to copy, with the means he
has at his disposal in the parish, the *models* that are given
to him for experimental celebrations: he is led to abandon
the traditional outlines of the liturgy to replace them with
new symbols, which, he thinks, will be appealing, insofar as they are directly intelligible to the faithful: directly
intelligible because they are modelled on the words and
gestures of everyday life, which are said to be meaningful.

Thus a person should shake hands with his neighbor
when the time comes to extend the sign of peace: it is
more convivial. Thus the children are asked to form a
circle around the altar at the time of the Our Father: it is
more charming. Thus the celebrant does his best to proclaim the prayers in a tone that is supposed to be more

---

[3] The two publications most used in [French] parishes to destabi-
lize the liturgy under the pretext of pastoral concerns are *Les Feuilles
liturgiques du diocèse de Saint-Brieuc* and *Signes d'aujourd'hui*.

intimate. Thus the altar is decorated with a bouquet of flowers and a single candle to give it the appearance of a table that has been prepared for a festive meal: it is less hieratic, as well as nicer. Thus the celebrant goes for a casual stroll in the aisles of the church just before Mass, to shake people's hands, while the liturgical animator takes the microphone and extends a *welcome to one and all* at the beginning of Mass and tells everyone to *have a good day* at the end of the celebration. This way the impression is given of being closer to people's *real-life experience*, and so on. These are just so many pastoral gimmicks that in the end quite simply pollute the liturgy of the Church.

As for the liturgical team entrusted with the task of developing a program for the Mass, it often digs into a repertoire of the latest, fashionable hymns. For example, it may choose a hit song heard at the latest concert: "How Beautiful Are Your Works", or a song that has been given media coverage on account of its emotional freight: Yves Duteil's "Take a Child by the Hand", which they use at Midnight Mass in some cases or at the funerals of young children . . . or there's the Irish Alleluia as well, which is reminiscent of the *cool* tunes that were in vogue during the hippie years.[4]

Unquestionably such choices turn Sunday celebrations into wild pendulum swings between a blaring fairground style and a style of sugary sweetness, between kitsch

---

[4] And what can we say about the success and popularity of that languorous pseudo-anamnesis, "Christ has come, Christ is born, . . ." and so on?

and mawkish sentimentality. The mawkish sentimentality makes its way to the fore when it comes time to play on the emotions (mainly at funeral Masses), and kitsch when it comes time to enhance the splendor of a ceremony (a pastoral visit from the bishop, for example). In these two instances, the absence of a noble simplicity leads to a desire to make the weight of emotion take precedence over the truth of liturgical forms; as well, though, this situation leads to the invention of Masses that are singularly lacking in unity, internal logic, and refinement.

2. *The place of emotions in the liturgy*

Thus, to make the Mass more attractive and more meaningful, liturgical animators play on the chords of sentiment and emotion. This is not a new phenomenon. Now in wanting to play on these kinds of responses, a person runs serious risks, for all emotions aim, in the first place, to produce a sense of turmoil that allows the will to be lulled to sleep.   ·

Thus, when one of the faithful is heard to declare, at the end of a celebration, "That was a beautiful Mass. I really liked it!", it must be understood that in using the adjective *beautiful* to describe the liturgy he has attended, this particular member of the faithful implies that what struck him first and foremost was a subjective emotion. In fact, he was stirred by what he was given to see and hear during the Mass: but this excitement, by paralyzing his judgment, caused him to lose sight of the primary, essential meaning that the celebration ought to have, a meaning that is made perceptible by the liturgy and is conveyed by it.[5]

Sadly, such a member of the faithful has utterly forgotten that, in the liturgy, *beauty* ought not to be the result of the talent of the celebrant or the liturgical team or the choir or indeed the animator. Liturgical *beauty* ought to remain something above the competence of the actors in a celebration, something above their talent, if they have any. Liturgical *beauty* resides in the fact that the sole aim of the priest when he celebrates is to want to do what the Church does. Since this is the case, the celebration is not merely *beautiful* in the human sense of the term: it is also *a good* in the theological sense of the term. And therein lies its essence, for it is this essential *good* from which true liturgical *beauty* proceeds.

But since we have all more or less lost a proper sense of the liturgy, we all too often confuse liturgical *beauty* with the aestheticism that is apt to come as a by-product of the whole notion of putting on a show that is external to the liturgy.[6]

3. The role of emotions

If emotions are capable of lulling the will to sleep by relying all too often on pathos to heighten the affective

---

[5] God is very much beyond the pleasurable thrills of our human nature, contrary to what certain romantics have been led to believe following Spinoza.

[6] Certainly, aesthetics has a place in the liturgy, but the liturgy does not derive its essential quality from aesthetics.

dimension, they are apt to disrupt the activity of the intelligence to the point where the member of the faithful can no longer succeed in giving a "subjective response to the objective nature of the liturgy".[7]

At that stage, the individual, having fallen victim to a kind of blindness, resorts to criticisms of the liturgy of the Church and then turns to transforming it in order to adapt it to his personal needs. Hence all those "stunted, limited" liturgies that we are forced to endure in our parishes. Hence those celebrations, stripped to their absolute minimum in terms of ritual, during which all you get are moralizing homilies and practical commentaries serving more often than not as an outlet by which certain types give vent to their personal problems.[8] So emotion is an infectious discord that must not be trusted: probably more so in the liturgy than elsewhere.[9]

---

[7] Cardinal Ratzinger, in *The Feast of Faith* (San Francisco: Ignatius Press, 1986), 68.

[8] We see, for example, the Christian meaning of Lent or Christmas often passed over in silence; all that counts is the charity practiced by any given charitable body whatsoever, as if this were enough to make everything all right.

[9] Popular piety has always been fostered by the emotions of the faithful; now this popular piety has its own significance in the life of the Church. But precisely because popular piety plays on the emotional feelings of individuals, Pope John Paul II asks for pastors to be prudent in this regard. In the letter issued for the twenty-fifth anniversary of the Council's Constitution on the Sacred Liturgy, *Vicesimus quintus annus* (December 4, 1988), no. 18, he writes: "Both the pious exercises of the Christian people and also other forms of devotion are welcomed and encouraged provided that they do not replace or intrude into liturgical celebrations. An authentic pastoral promotion of the Liturgy will

Now all too often it is the emotions that are pursued in the exercise of certain extraordinary liturgical functions: *doing* the readings, directing the singing, distributing communion, and so on. Many pastors still do not want to acknowledge or admit that, in asking laymen to fulfill a liturgical function, they have fostered, in certain individuals in search of inner peace or yearning for affection, the gratification of sentiments that have been mistakenly confused with a state of spiritual well-being.[10] Confusing such sentiments with genuine consolations of the Holy Spirit is an utterly erroneous way of viewing genuine spiritual development.

Consequently, it must in fact be seen that a priest who invites a member of the lay faithful to help out with the liturgy and thereby fosters this sort of confusion in him is seriously guilty of a lack of discernment and prudence.[11] Indeed, to conduct affairs in such a way that a member

---

build upon the riches of popular piety, purifying and directing them towards the Liturgy as the offering of the peoples."

[10] Perhaps it is for this reason as well that the *Instruction on Certain Questions Regarding the Collaboration of the Non-Ordained Faithful in the Sacred Ministry of Priests* (August 15, 1997) has had a poor reception, especially in France and Germany: people realized that the instruction required certain basic questions to be asked.

[11] All the more because it cannot always be known what the real motivations of the priest who "calls" a layman to the service of the liturgy are: does he not sometimes do it in order to create a relationship of complicity that allows him to revel in a feeling of security through tacit, sub-verbal relationships that have been established precisely by means of the liturgy? (On this delicate question, see *Instruction on Certain Questions Regarding the Collaboration of the Non-Ordained Faithful in the Sacred Ministry of Priests*, particularly article 6, paragraph 2, where the matter

of the faithful can accord himself gratifying sentiments by exercising a liturgical function, when in point of fact his real vocation does not correspond to that function, amounts to fostering in him "a kind of mental schizophrenia that can also lead to psychic disturbance and, at times, to moral deviations" that end up sooner or later affecting the atmosphere of the parish community.[12]

So anything that would allow an individual to claim the liturgy for himself in order to feather his own nest with it must be carefully avoided,[13] whether this be done consciously or unconsciously on the part of persons who are psychologically fragile.[14]

---

in question is the confusion that can be engendered by "anomalous liturgical practices").

[12] Congregation for the Doctrine of the Faith, *Letter to the Bishops of the Catholic Church on Some Aspects of Christian Meditation*, (October 15, 1989), no. 28.

[13] This would cause them to fall prey to a new form of the syndrome that in former days was called "being a Holy Joe".

[14] Saint Benedict seems to give prudent instructions by way of safeguard, so that the oratory and the liturgical world that relates to it may not become secure little "nests". In his Rule he says: "We must know that God regards our purity of heart and tears of compunction, not our many words. Prayer [what he is talking about here is personal prayer] should therefore be short and pure, unless perhaps it is prolonged under the inspiration of divine grace. In community, however, prayer should always be brief; and when the superior gives the signal, all should rise together" (*The Rule of Saint Benedict in English* [Collegeville, Minn.: Liturgical Press, 1982], chap. 20). And he goes on to say: "The oratory ought to be what it is called, and nothing else is to be done or stored there. After the Work of God, all should leave in complete silence and with reverence for God" (ibid.). Saint Benedict stresses two points: the shortness of prayer and the fact that the oratory should be left as

4. *"Pleasurable disorders"*

Thus, any liturgy that gives rise among the faithful to "pleasurable disorders",[15] by whatever manner of means,[16]

---

soon as the liturgy is finished. So Saint Benedict shows, in an implicit way, that when liturgical prayer is done as it should be done, nothing should be added; when it is finished, you have to know how to sever all ties and stand back from the "warm atmosphere" of the liturgy. Any refusal to break with the pleasant atmosphere of the liturgy leads to the creation of paraliturgies, which run the risk, in certain cases, of inducing false, dysfunctional patterns of behavior.

[15] A "pleasurable disorder" is the ambiguous pleasure caused by the fact that a person believes he has found a compensation for the loss of a real or symbolic object. This object has to do with a "first love" (in the sense of a fusional attachment), and a person has to be able to break free of it, inasmuch as it is marked by a bond that is more possessive than it is selfless. In many instances, the fact of securing an extraordinary ministry in the liturgy is a compensation of this kind: that is why in the ranks of female liturgical animators you are often apt to find single women (widowed or divorced) whereas among male liturgical animators you can often find former seminarians. In both instances, it appears that these people cannot manage to accept the loss of the object of their first love and to undertake what psychologists call "the grieving process" (cf. J. F. Catalan, *Expérience spirituelle et psychologie* [Desclée de Brouwer, 1993]; *L'Homme et sa religion* [Desclée de Brouwer, 1994]).

[16] Even as a person is justified in showing prudence in the way he looks upon the celebrations of certain charismatic groups that have a tendency to lay too much stress on the outward expression of their feelings, similarly there must be some measure of reservation shown toward those of the faithful who like Latin Masses only for emotional reasons or who would introduce Gregorian chant into the liturgy only for sentimental reasons. (A priest who falls into this category, for example, celebrates Mass without any regard for liturgical norms, but "wants" some Gregorian chant, since, he says, this reminds him of his time in the seminary, when he was specifically chosen for his beau-

is a dangerous celebration insofar as it generates false behavior and prevents the faithful from overcoming traits
in their own personality.

Obviously it is not a case of underestimating our feelings and emotions: it is a case, first, of controlling them.
Everyone has his own particular problems and frailties;
but some people are fortunate in being better endowed
than others when it comes to the difficult conquest of
themselves. So knowing this, let us not use the liturgy to
compound the problem: let us not pamper our neuroses
by devising or choosing liturgical rites to suit ourselves,
rites that allow us to play false roles![17]

In the same way, let us be suspicious with regard to
anything that is apt to have a romantic coloring in the
liturgy:[18] for in playing on the feelings and emotions, ro-

---

tiful voice. Even so, this priest may confess that he is not concerned
which pieces ought to be sung on any given Sunday: the important
thing is that it be Gregorian chant. He would just as soon sing the
Dirigatur gradual every Sunday of the year, since it was the piece he
liked best when he was a seminarian. Here we have an example of the
way in which not only Gregorian chant, but the liturgy itself, can be
subverted.)

[17] Cf. Albert Memmi, "Les Délices empoissonnés", in *Le Figaro*.

[18] There have been several periods of romanticism in the course of
the centuries: the gothic style or the baroque style, for example, could
be construed as expressions of a certain sort of romanticism; but a controlled romanticism, insofar as it was able to submit to precise rules.
When the gothic style (which is a spirit of enthusiasm) thought it could
free itself from the rules that imposed moderation and limits on it, it
lapsed into the flamboyant style. Similarly, the baroque style turned
into the rococo. Flamboyant and rococo were signs, as it were, of an
imminent decadence, inasmuch as they were more reliant on a kind of
mad obsession on the part of artists than on the truth of forms.

manticism has all too often been the source of serious misunderstandings and profound unrest.

The liturgy must not be transformed into an emotion machine: to let oneself be led by emotions that others incite by subverting the liturgy in order to render it more meaningful is really tantamount to agreeing not to be entirely oneself. It is playing a game that has been rigged by the person who has been given the power[19] to intensify one's passions.

On the contrary, when the liturgy is correctly performed according to the rites that have been tested by tradition and therefore recognized by the Church, it allows the individual to structure himself: it shows him his true place by giving him at one and the same time both his status as an individual and his social status; it protects him from possible pathological components of the group into which he has integrated himself in order to participate in divine praise; it channels and controls the current that carries the member of the faithful into the presence of spiritual realities.

So there are great dangers in wanting to break free of the rites given by the Church: the danger of handing one's mind over to disorder, vagrancy, or intellectual paralysis.

---

[19] Often by the institution that has given him unbridled power.

Why it is necessary for the liturgy to be ritualized

1. Useful emotions

In his apostolic letter *Orientale lumen*, issued on May 2, 1995, John Paul II teaches that the Eastern liturgy allows "an integral development of the person in his rational and emotional components". So, together with the Pope, we should accept and understand that the capacity to be moved by the emotions is part of the richness of the human person. Does this assertion manage to contradict everything that has been said above? It all depends, of course, on the meaning that we attach to the emotions.

When a person speaks of the emotions, it must be understood, to be sure, that there do exist useful emotions. There are the emotions, for example, that urge us to act in the face of danger in order to save someone, even though our intelligence urges us to take flight instead.[20] There are also ones that dictate the way we ought to behave toward the person we love. These kinds of emotions are signals.

Emotion can give rise to love: but must love necessarily make a person blind, as the saying goes? Must emotion necessarily lead into the troubled waters of a reckless, disordered passion? Thus we understand quite well that to be truly fruitful and liberating, emotion has to be constantly controlled, constantly questioned.

---

[20] At the present time some specialists are speaking in terms of "emotional intelligence".

2. The control that is necessary over the emotions

Every emotion is a signal that must always be interpreted. And after having been interpreted, it must be able to be controlled in such a way that it does not lead to acting in an anarchic or impetuous way. Having a pain somewhere is a signal: this signal must be interpreted by the doctor so that, having discovered the diseased organ, he can dispense the appropriate medicine. Similarly, emotion is a message that has to be deciphered.

Now in the case of the liturgy, it is precisely the ritual element that allows the emotions to be at once controlled and dominated. The person who abolishes the rituals or subverts them comes quickly to use the emotions to transform celebrations into shows, into liturgical entertainment during which he himself plays the actor. Together with the other participants, he comes to share in a kind of collective hysteria, not unlike what happens when thousands of young people gather together around star personalities in show business.[21]

Liturgical ritual allows our emotions to be controlled only insofar as it goes beyond us and is not the result of a personal, subjective construction, but is the fruit of the Church's experience.

---

[21] This is only a short step away from having people flick on their lighters and hold them out at arm's length, so that they can wave their flames in unison. Are these the lengths to which we are willing to go in our Sunday Masses in order "to please people"?

3. *Liturgical rites and the building of the personality*

The liturgy allows the emotions to be controlled and the self to be structured because, such as it is given to us by the Church, with her perfectly codified rituals, it is the result of a long, balancing process of maturation achieved through contact with a living and purifying tradition. This tradition has caused the liturgy to be developed according to what man is in his essence, according to his psychology and to what he can truly understand and feel.

Even while integrating the constituent parts of our humanity over the centuries, by aiming to express them through sound, moderate rituals,[22] the liturgy has been engaged in a constant process of selection in order that the attitudes expressing the sacred may not be distorted by what is deviant and weak in our humanity as well.[23]

---

[22] The rites we see being performed during the liturgy do not have to be expressed in words (explained and commented on): their sole accomplishment is a guarantee of orthodoxy and at the same time a landmark that helps us to be what we ought to be within the framework of redeemed creation.

[23] "A highly developed society has many significant, often complex, forms. If it wants to maintain its cultural level, it should, in the education it gives its children, attend carefully to teaching them how to handle these forms and especially how to comprehend their immaterial significance, something that will be all the easier insofar as the visible form being used is one of quality. Another remarkable quality of significant forms is that not only do they allow the transmission to others of intellectual or spiritual goods, but they also help the person who uses them practically to deepen the consciousness he has of their nonmaterial finality. Finally, a rudimentary part of the original, functional form may be sufficient in itself to convey the sign: a simple handshake instead

That is why the Church has regularly been obliged to conduct a critical examination of her liturgical rites: at the Council of Trent, as at Vatican II, she eliminated from the liturgy aspects that ran the risk of nurturing emotions likely to engender feelings of guilt or anxiety among some of the faithful, or also behavior patterns of an obsessional nature; it abolished "elements . . . that are out of harmony with the inner nature of the liturgy", [24] even though these elements may have had their value at a certain period.

Progressive Catholics who constantly manipulate the liturgy to make it, according to their way of thinking, more accessible and more meaningful do not seem to have perceived that the world of the liturgy is not without its dangers: the Church, with her "expertise in human nature" [25] is well aware of this, and this is why, over the centuries, she has codified the liturgy by specifying the rites to be performed. The rite is precisely the "tool" [26]

---

of an embrace, an obelisk instead of a complete building. The condition sine qua non is that the original functionality has disappeared. When a person drinks a toast, he lifts his glass and is content to take just a sip without quenching his thirst" (Prof. Jan Boogaarts, vice-president of the Vatican's International Center for Sacred Music, in *Actes du IIe Colloque d'études historiques, théologiques et canoniques sur le rite catholique romain* [CIEL, October 1996]).

[24] SC 21.

[25] To use a phrase employed by Paul VI and repeated by John Paul II.

[26] The rite must be taken for what it is and must not be given importance it does not have: you cannot believe in liturgical rites to the point of letting yourself be caught up in them. In reality, it is advisable to look on rites with a certain detachment—with a certain humor even —in order to be able to get beyond them. You have to believe in them enough to give yourself over to them completely, to respect them, and

that allows the liturgy not to deviate and not to cause the faithful to deviate, insofar as the error—if there is error —is not in the liturgy[27] but in man.

Fidelity to the liturgical rites established by the Church is the guarantee that the liturgical celebration is going to express the indescribable with the help of sound, "super-significant" forms and is not going to limit itself merely to playing with the passion-charged states of individuals.

When the officially established rites are lacking, then the liturgy becomes deviant: it progressively entraps the mind in the changing, unrestrained emotions of those who are in charge of implementing it.

Now anything that thus affects our way of thinking has repercussions on the body; the body reacts by adopting false patterns of behavior, as well as attitudes and gestures that can become questionable insofar as they begin to signify something utterly different from what the liturgy wishes to convey and to create a gulf between the *lex orandi* and the *lex credendi*.

But the liturgy is also and especially the common good of the whole Church; for this reason, nobody can consider himself to be a proprietor of the rites. Modifying the rites in order to give the liturgy a more personal style always carries with it the danger of developing a subjective piety that can eventually lay bare the disorder that

---

to perform them with dignity, but at the same time not too much, in order to be able to preserve your freedom and not risk lapsing into a ritualism that is as paralyzing to the body as it is to the mind.

[27] The liturgy is a theological locus par excellence: what the Church believes is celebrated by means of the liturgy.

sin has introduced into the harmony of the human being.[28] In that case the meaning of the liturgy changes:
no longer characterized as *ex opere operato*, no longer expressive of the real, mystical presence of Christ, but only
as the *ex opere operantis* aspect, that is to say, the fervor
of the congregation that has been stimulated artificially
with the help of well-calculated liturgies that serve only to
gain sway over the affective consciousness of the participants.

Certainly people are sincere, and what they do is not
necessarily theatrical play-acting; but worship and a personal relationship with God by way of the sacrifice of the
Cross are nonetheless minimized. The only things that
count and that are glorified are the mutual relations that
exist among men and their social bonds: sharing, communion, dialogue. All of this falls under the heading of
mere effusive sentiment, even if it is genuine: Do you
have to be a Catholic to engage in this sort of thing?

Under such a guiding vision of reality, it comes to be
understood that obeying liturgical rules is no longer necessary: thus genuine signs of the sacred should be replaced
by personal initiative or the creativity of the group that
has gathered together to celebrate.

It is precisely this approach that is rejected by the faithful, who understand instinctively, it may be said, that this

---

[28] Cf. John Paul II, letter *Dominicae cenae*, To All the Bishops of the
Church on the Mystery and Worship of the Eucharist (February 24,
1980), no. 12; the apostolic letter *Orientale lumen* (May 2, 1995), no.
11.

evolutionary liturgy must necessarily lead to the creation of new creeds and the development of new eucharistic prayers: which leaves the door open to gnosis.[29]

---

[29] See the very exhaustive study made by Gérard Soulages in *Épreuves chrétiennes et espérance* (Paris: Téqui, 1979).

CHAPTER NINE

What Does the Future Hold
for the Roman Liturgy?

After having assessed the present situation[1] and after having shown the errors made by both sides in this issue, is it possible to imagine solutions that would allow an end to the corruptions visited on the Roman liturgy?

Responding to an investigation made by *La Nef*[2] that dealt with the preconciliar liturgy, Cardinal Angelo Felici, president of the pontifical commission *Ecclesia Dei*, writes as follows: "What must be noted is that there are still too many erroneous interpretations and arbitrary implementations when it comes to doctrine, liturgy, and discipline. These sorts of things have not yet been rejected everywhere, as is insistently demanded by the motu proprio; but nevertheless it is precisely these abuses that are the root cause of the dissatisfaction felt by many of the faithful."

So it is clear that, if the Roman liturgy appears these days to be utterly coming apart at the seams and if in many instances it seems to be a complete shambles, it is

---

[1] Denis Crouan, *The Liturgy Betrayed* (San Francisco: Ignatius Press, 2000).

[2] *Enquête sur la messe traditionnelle*, special issue no. 6 of *La Nef* (1998).

in large part due to the lack of discipline of some and the ignorance of many others concerning what was said and desired by the Council.

So it would not be without merit to suppose that, in order to put an end to the liturgical crisis, there are two action plans that need to be considered and undertaken jointly: an action plan based on an attitude of rejection and, on the other hand, an action plan aimed at rebuilding. In fact, "we are no longer in a time of sober discretion, but in a time of confrontation. . . . Some men remain in the Church in order to change her and some in order to destroy her",[3] and this planned program of destruction, as we well know, is implemented in many places by the imposition of a falsified liturgy.

An attitude of rejection

Today we have come to realize that, even immediately after Vatican II, the issue has been confused by pseudo-theologians, questionable exegetes, and, it must be added, by numerous militants who have been given a great deal too much in the way of responsibility. These members of the faithful—clergy as well as laymen—"well-meaning perhaps but equipped with a very rudimentary knowledge of theology and to whom a sense of the sacred and a sense of beauty are all too foreign",[4] have preferred to follow

---

[3] Cardinal Journet as quoted by Gérard Soulages, *Épreuves chrétiennes et espérance* (Paris: Téqui, 1979).

[4] Bishop Bernard Dupire, a lecture given at the Solesmes Symposium of Associations for the Roman Liturgy in Latin.

blindly every passing fad rather than be obedient to the prudent directives of their superiors.

It is true that there was much talk at that point about pluralism and the right to free speech in the Church; these slogans allowed all manner of novel experiments to be justified in the name of the spirit of the Council. The bishops should have immediately been suspicious of this sudden taste for a pluralism, which was destined in very short order to be revealed as an explosive factor in parish communities and eucharistic assemblies: Was it not obvious that the libertarian spirit whereby some people gave themselves leave to disregard the directives given by the Roman Missal "would have repercussions on faith, the moral law, and the essential framework of the sacraments, the liturgy, and canonical discipline, which tend to preserve the unity that is necessary in the Church"? Was it not obvious that it was going to put the foundations of the Creed in question?[5]

It is true that some bishops began to intervene more often. But it is recognized these days that they were often quite timid and in particular much too collective—or collegial—at a time when the faithful would have preferred each individual bishop to have the courage to act effectively, on his own authority, in order to rectify the errors that were growing ever more numerous in the parishes of his own diocese.

Unfortunately, all too often it did not turn out this way in the climate of uncertainty and experimentation that followed the Council, at a time when everyone pro-

---

[5] Paul VI, allocution of October 27, 1969.

posed his own interpretation of Vatican II to legitimize all the experiments in the areas of liturgy and catechesis: all too many of the bishops showed themselves to be over-cautious and excessively timid and, in the statements they made, took on the guise of simple, ordinary "men, whose opinions people were free to accept or reject".[6]

During this postconciliar period there was no shortage of opinions. They were formulated in the first place by theologians who, on the pretext of "academic freedom" and "the openness of the Council", circulated ideas that were in total contradiction to the traditional teaching of the Church, even though Vatican II had demanded insistently that it should be kept intact.

These opinions were then accepted by the all too numerous bureaucratic bodies created after the Council, to which the bishops had given their entire confidence with a disarming naïveté that prevented them from seeing reality.

Now the reality was that, in these bureaucratic bodies as a whole, the experts and people in charge became entrenched and in this way found the opportunity to join forces—aided and abetted by the powerful financial means at their disposal—so as to establish themselves as a veritable parallel magisterium, arrogating to themselves all power over the liturgy, catechesis,[7] the so-called Catholic press, the activities of Catholic Action, and the con-

---

[6] Cardinal F. Marty, archbishop of Paris, allocution to the French Conference of Bishops at Lourdes, October 3, 1973.

[7] People still remember the "*Pierres vivantes*" controversy, in which Rome asked the bishops to revise their material.

tent of religious broadcasts on television and radio, and so on.

What is more, these bureaucratic bodies were taken over by influential members of diocesan priests' councils, who were charged with naming parish priests; consequently, the priest who was faithful to the Council was sent to the most progressive parishes, where he ended up being psychologically demolished, whereas the most progressive priest was sent to areas that had remained traditional, where, with the help of teams of lay people, he could undertake the task of demolishing the parishes that had been entrusted to him.

The diocesan authorities whom the faithful approached in order to point out the damage done by certain pastors remained by and large silent: in the end it was not the arsonist who became the object of resentment, but the person who rang the alarm to sound a warning about the danger.[8]

Nevertheless, had Paul VI himself not rung the alarm when he declared: "From among our own selves, as in the time of Saint Paul, have arisen men speaking perverse things, to draw away the disciples after them" (Acts 20:30)?

Unfortunately, to add to the confusion, all manner of questioning and protest against the doctrine and teaching of the Magisterium was often presented at the time as a sign of the vitality of the postconciliar Church, whereas any form of obedience to the Pope was looked on as

---

[8] Cf. André Frossard, *Le Parti de Dieu; lettre ouverte aux évêques* (Paris: Fayard, 1992).

narrow-minded. It was a time when, in the diocesan seminaries, future priests were encouraged to compose their own Mass prayers and devise new eucharistic prayers; those who wanted to respect the Roman Missal were reproached for being too rigid, not open enough to the pastoral aspects of theology; singing the least little bit of Gregorian chant was forbidden. "Let's leave the past behind and start anew with a clean slate": such was the slogan that seemed to have been adopted in most houses of religious formation, including seminaries regarded by the faithful as staunchly classical.[9]

Faced with the distortions that had been made of Vatican II and the errors that had been conveyed about the teaching of the Council, some bishops often remained as if paralyzed. At least that was the unpleasant impression they conveyed to many of the bewildered faithful.

How many pastors declared that they did not know about the doctrinal errors in their diocese and the Masses that were constantly being celebrated in violation of the norms, even though they were kept completely informed by a large number of scandalized, wounded parishioners?[10]

How many bishops confessed that they could not or

---

[9] In one such seminary, considered "classical" as compared with other diocesan seminaries, the bishop permitted the practice of intercommunion between Protestants and Catholics and let certain theologians teach against the dogma of the Real Presence.

[10] Just one example among many: in a certain parish, a woman religious in civilian dress concelebrates every Sunday with the priest. Three bishops in succession have held the helm of the diocese in which this parish is located; all three of them were informed of this grave irregularity, but none of them reacted to it. Cf. as well André Mignot and Michel de Saint Pierre, *Les Fumées de Satan* (Paris: Table Ronde, 1976).

would not intervene directly to put an end to certain abuses they had knowledge of, so significant was the power of diocesan and national bureaucracies?[11]

Nevertheless, it was when Cardinal Marty warned his brother bishops to be on guard against the danger of appearing "mute and paralyzed" that Paul VI recalled that the responsibility of the bishop is "of a personal nature and absolutely inalienable, so that he may respond to the immediate, day to day needs of the People of God."[12]

Would it not be a good thing if today's bishops plucked up the courage to make clear-cut choices and adopted, if need be, a firm "attitude of refusal"[13] in the face of anything that could be construed as a distortion of the liturgy that stems from the restoration desired by Vatican II? This way diocesan pastors could put a stop to the recurring errors of the past and spare themselves a reproach for a silence that could be regarded as fear or weakness.

Such an attitude would allow the faithful to regain once more the landmarks that are utterly lacking today in the area of liturgy: thus they could rediscover their taste for the true prayer of the Church, by coming indeed to understand that it is not the constitution *Sacrosanctum concilium* of Vatican II that is the cause of the current crisis, but

---

[11] So, in desperation, many of the faithful went directly to the Holy See, an action that—as can easily be understood and imagined—was hardly palatable to the diocesan bishops. (On this subject, see an eloquent statement of the archdiocese of Rennes after the publication of the *Instruction on Certain Questions Regarding the Collaboration of the Non-Ordained Faithful in the Sacred Ministry of Priests*, August 15, 1997).

[12] Maurice Angibaud, *Le Démon dans l'Église* (Résiac, 1977).

[13] The words are those of John Paul II (cf. motu proprio *Ecclesia Dei adflicta*).

the way in which this conciliar document has for too long been used and distorted by various groups, of whatever stripe in the political spectrum.[14]

It would also be a good thing if all diocesan or national publications that openly betray the Council by putting forward illegitimate adaptations of the current Roman Missal were dismissed out of hand. Such publications, whose sole function is to make their authors rich by ruining the liturgy, have not received any official recognition or sanction from the Church; they merely serve as an alibi for celebrants and liturgical teams that fabricate and impose phony, disgraceful styles of liturgical celebration, ridden with idiosyncracies, which the majority of the faithful no longer care for, if, that is, they ever did in the first place.

Next it would be a good thing if there were a rejection of all Masses that, even though they are celebrated in normal conditions that are conducive to the proper use of the prescribed rites, do not respect the right of the faithful to the true liturgy as defined in the current Roman Missal. The Roman Missal that was published in the wake of Vatican II gives the outline of a typical Mass: it is this Mass that every member of the faithful ought to be able to find anywhere. It is the liturgical norm to be followed,[15] but who out there knows this?

"A certain measure of respect is owed to the Christian people. The Code of Canon Law is quite insistent about

---

[14] Cf. Father Michel Lelong, in *Enquête sur la messe traditionnelle*.

[15] See *The General Instruction of the Roman Missal* (2000), chap. 4, heading I A, nos. 120ff.

this: Christians have the right to have a liturgy that is the liturgy of the Church and not the whim of the celebrant or local pastor", as Bishop Lagrange has most properly reminded us.[16]

Would these emergency measures not make it possible to nip the burgeoning growth of a more or less anarchic multi-ritualism, which is what the bishops seem to be afraid of at present[17] and which is, in point of fact, already widespread?

In a communication addressed to Bishop Ré, Mr. de Saventhem noted:[18]

What the faithful are assisting at are innumerable different forms of eucharistic celebrations, which have been proliferating in the Church for twenty-five years and which draw their inspiration with more or less legitimacy from various *national editions* of the Roman Missal of Paul VI[19] and the multiple *options* that they make provision for.[20] And in many cases these celebrations utterly lack a legitimate basis, so that the Congregation for Divine Worship

---

[16] In *Enquête sur la messe traditionnelle.*

[17] Cf. Bishop Jean-Charles Thomas, bishop of Versailles, about the coexistence of two rites, which is what the traditionalist movements want, in ibid.

[18] Letter of May 24, 1994, in ibid.

[19] It is in order to note here that Mr. de Saventhem, president of the Una Voce Federation, concedes that the so-called Missal of Paul VI is indeed a Roman Missal, a fact that is still denied by certain collaborators of Una Voce who persist in describing the liturgy defined by the Missal of Paul VI as a *new rite.*

[20] What many celebrants are unaware of is that options—which are in fact provided for in the current Roman Missal—only have meaning and legitimacy when a person has first faithfully sought to implement what is provided for by the norms. An option that becomes a rule makes no more sense than a norm that becomes the exception.

has been forced to admit that they "constitute notable elements of division for the faithful, and this adds to their
illegitimacy" (*Notitiae*, 1992, no. 10, pp. 627–28).[21]

The gist of the matter is clear, and the analysis could not
be sounder; we would not be remiss in drawing the req-
uisite conclusions from this.

An attitude of reconstruction

The liturgy! Everybody speaks about it, writes about it,
and discusses the subject. It has been commented on, it
has been praised, and it has been criticized. But who really knows the principles and norms by which it is to be
put into practice? The constitution *Sacrosanctum concilium*
referred to the liturgy as the fountain and summit of the
life of the Church (no. 10): What is being done to make
this sublime definition become reality?

These were the terms in which, on October 17, 1985,
Pope John Paul II addressed members of the Congregation for Divine Worship and the Discipline of the Sacraments.

---

[21] Mr. de Saventhem adds: "As for the reception accorded to such
celebrations, it must not be forgotten that in most parishes they have
quite simply been imposed and that the faithful in their discouragement
have had no other means of 'rejecting' them than by a silent turning
away. Which explains, to a great extent at least, the catastrophic col-
lapse in attendance at Sunday services. As is noted again by the Congregation for Divine Worship: 'After thirty years of unhomogeneous
implementation, the credibility of the reform has been jeopardized.'
And the Congregation compares the current state of affairs to what
usually results when 'institutions are sapped by internal divisions: loss
of credibility, disaffection toward the institution in question, and finally estrangement and loss of contact.' "

Ten years later, Cardinal Ratzinger wrote: "I am convinced that the crisis in the Church that we are experiencing today is to a large extent due to the disintegration of the liturgy, which at times has even come to be conceived of *etsi Deus non daretur*: in that it is a matter of indifference whether or not God exists and whether or not he speaks to us and hears us."[22]

Thus, more than thirty years after Vatican II, it must indeed be conceded that the number of people dissatisfied with the state in which the Roman liturgy finds itself is constantly growing: the works that have been published recently dealing with liturgical problems stand as proof positive of this.[23] While some people are still questioning the constitution *Sacrosanctum concilium*, others, who have become more and more numerous, do not hesitate rather to criticize its improper implementation.

Be this as it may, the problems that persist, and which are getting worse by reason of their persistence, are reflected in the life of the Church and the faith life of members of the faithful, inasmuch as an attenuated understanding of the meaning of the liturgy goes hand in hand with a more or less pronounced weakening of the Christian life itself.

The work of rebuilding the liturgy, which is impera-

---

[22] Joseph Cardinal Ratzinger, *Milestones: Memoirs 1927–1977*, trans. Erasmo Leiva-Merikakis (San Francisco: Ignatius Press, 1998), 148–49.

[23] Claude Barthe, *Reconstruire la liturgie* (Paris: F. X. de Guibert; C. Geffroy and P. Maxence, in *Enquête sur la messe traditionnelle*; interview with Father Hage and Denis Crouan in *L'Homme nouveau* (Paris: Place Saint-Sulpice), August 1998.

tive today, should take its inspiration from a four-point program:

— theological formation

— a rediscovery of the sacred

— the importance given to the aesthetic dimension of the liturgy

— an abandonment of the privatization of the liturgy

1. Theological formation

From almost the very beginning of the text of the constitution *Sacrosanctum concilium*, there is an insistence on the necessity for a complete and serious formation: "Mother Church earnestly desires that all the faithful be led to that full, conscious, and active participation in liturgical celebrations. . . . In the restoration and promotion of the sacred liturgy, this full and active participation by all the people is the aim to be considered before all else."[24]

But, the conciliar text goes on to add immediately, there is no hope of obtaining such a result without preliminary training. These days everyone can see that, while the notion of participation enjoys widespread currency —which is quite praiseworthy in itself—the notion of serious training and formation has, on the other hand, been utterly forgotten.

The constitution *Sacrosanctum concilium*, however, spec-

---

[24] SC 14.

ifies with the greatest of clarity who should be formed and what the proper basis for formation is. First and foremost, formation should be aimed at professors who are appointed to teach liturgy in seminaries and theological faculties.[25] After that it should be aimed at the clergy themselves. They should tackle liturgical questions in their theological, pastoral, historical, spiritual, and juridical aspects, in order to gain an understanding of sacred rites and in order to learn how to observe liturgical norms in their celebrations.[26]

Finally, the lay faithful should in their turn be allowed to benefit from a true formation; this ought to be done "with zeal and patience", as the text of the Council goes on to point out. This formation intended for laymen should not take place in a way that focuses on their sensibilities—for, contrary to what is often maintained nowadays, the liturgy is not so much a question of sensibilities as a principle of truth—but it should be done with an attitude of respect for their age and their state of life, as well as their level of religious culture. Thus liturgical formation presupposes an adaptive catechesis that is distinct from the liturgy itself.[27]

These should have been the ends and means of a pastoral approach to the liturgy that was desired by the Council: a pastoral approach that today needs to be devised and implemented as soon as possible, so that it may allow the

---

[25] SC 15.
[26] SC 16–18.
[27] John Paul II, apostolic letter *Dies Domini* (May 31, 1998), no. 36.

liturgy "to lead the faithful to love, adoration, and praise for the Father, as well as contemplative silence".[28]

We have to concede that for a host of reasons, to which allusion was made above, the "serious" formation required by Vatican II has not been adequately ensured everywhere. It is well known that even to this day, in numerous seminaries and institutes, the liturgy has a second-rate status in the formation given to future priests. Furthermore, in the majority of parishes, the faithful have an utterly false idea of the liturgy, since they only know it by way of the quirky, uncertain Sunday celebrations they find imposed on them, which stray to a greater or lesser degree from the regulations for liturgical celebration that are given by the Missal.[29]

2. A rediscovery of the sacred

During an allocution delivered on April 19, 1967, to the Council for the Liturgy, Paul VI did not hesitate to issue a stern warning against the willingness to desacralize the liturgy. The Sovereign Pontiff noted that this new tendency was laying the foundations for the destruction of authentic Catholic worship by introducing disruptions into doctrine and discipline as well as pastoral theology. Desacralization, he declared, poses the threat of spiritual ruin.

---

[28] John Paul II, apostolic letter *Vicesimus quintus annus*, (December 4, 1988).

[29] Which a certain number of bishops are beginning to recognize today.

Desacralizing the liturgy, that is to say, refusing to separate it from anything that could be construed as being trite and commonplace, leads to a denial in progressive stages of the distinction between ordinary bread and eucharistic bread. It is to admit little by little that, during the eucharistic meal, a person can be quite content to eat and drink without really distinguishing the Body and the Blood of Christ. Now the Apostle Paul teaches us that "any one who eats and drinks without discerning the body eats and drinks judgment upon himself" (1 Cor 11:29). Thus, for the Christian, the distinctions arising from the sacred are of capital importance: it could indeed be said that they are a question of life and death.

In order properly to show the differentiated, separate, sacred character of the eucharistic species, Christians have given themselves spaces that are distinct from profane places, as well as times that are distinct from the ordinariness of everyday life. They have surrounded the celebration of the Eucharist with rituals and ceremonies whose goal it is to highlight its extraordinary character. These allow the faithful to prepare themselves psychologically, in order that they may pass without violence from the world of the profane to the world of divine mystery.

Thus it is an essential function of the sacred to demonstrate the nature of a world that is in communion with God: it shows us the existence of a reality that is radically distinct from the ordinariness of a fallen world that has been given over to death and whose links to its Creator have been severed.

For all these reasons, we need to rediscover in today's

world that, in every liturgical celebration, the signs, gestures, actions, attitudes, words, objects, art, vestments, and spaces should be perceived, not as realities invented by the actors in the liturgy, but as "epiphanies", which is to say "revelations" of both the sacred and the divine, which stand outside of us but with which we are called to enter into communion.

Thus it is essential to avoid the development of liturgies that appear too much like catechetical tools or purely convivial affairs: liturgies imbued with superfluous commentaries, pointless entertainment, restless bustle around the altar and microphones.[30] All of this reinforces the belief that such celebrations proceed from a purely functional mode of thought. What can be seen over time is that this sort of functional approach leads, on the part of those who promote it, to a real degeneration of spiritual gifts and aptitudes, the end result of which is to alienate the faithful from the liturgy.[31]

3. The aesthetic dimension of the liturgy

Over the last few years, the noticeable weakening of the sense of the sacred has led to a loss of the aesthetic dimension of the liturgy. As a result there has been a veritable abandonment of the notion of splendor in liturgical ceremonies. A direct consequence of this is that many of the faithful feel that the values expressed in the past by

---

[30] Cf. Father Michel Lelong, in *Enquête sur la messe traditionnelle*.
[31] Cf. H. B. Meyer, *Was Kirchenbau bedeutet* (Fribourg/Basel/Vienne, 1984).

the traditional rites of the preconciliar liturgy have been lost.

Thus we have reached the point where the celebrations that are produced have begun to bear more and more resemblance to "a bad show that's not worth going to", to use the expression of Cardinal Danneels. Hence the present "discontent of many of the faithful who are turning to chapels run by the Fraternity of Saint Pius X and even to groups that are undoubtedly outside the Catholic Church".[32]

Even though it is difficult to define good taste[33] where the liturgy is concerned, care must be taken that every celebration is marked by an "aesthetic dimension that is essential, insofar as it allows man to perceive the beauty of what is being celebrated".[34]

In what way can the aesthetic dimension of the liturgy be recovered and turned to good account? All that is needed to achieve this is a willingness to implement the instructions given by the official texts of the Church. What are these instructions? The first of them is to be found in the constitution *Sacrosanctum concilium*. In the chapter that deals with the relationship between art and the liturgy, the text of the Council makes it clear that, in order to favor and promote a truly sacred art, there must be an attachment to "noble beauty" rather than mere extravagance.[35] In other words, it is not necessarily costly,

---

[32] Cf. Cardinal A. Felici, in *Enquête sur la messe traditionnelle*.

[33] See Denis Crouan, *L'Art et la liturgie* (Paris: Téqui).

[34] Congregation for the Clergy, *Directory for the Ministry and Life of Permanent Deacons*, Vatican 1998 (cf. no. 30).

[35] Cf. no. 124.

external pomp and ceremony, added in order to introduce a tone of artificial splendor, that confer a beauty on divine worship, but rather the way it is conducted practically, the delicacy that is shown in order to fulfill, in a faithful and orderly way, what is required by the liturgy of the Church.

The second instruction is in the *General Instruction of the Roman Missal*.[36] Tackling the question of the objects and furniture that should decorate the sanctuary of churches and that should serve to help in implementing the liturgy (altar, cross, chairs, credence table, ambo, candles, and so on), the Missal declares that "all these elements . . . should . . . form a deep and organic unity".[37]

Thus, the real beauty that belongs to the liturgy and that proceeds necessarily from having an educated sense of the sacred should be perceptible through our rejection of coarse vulgarity, of whatever is casual and disparate, and whatever risks appearing unbalanced, whether this be the result of omission or excess.

These days this kind of bad taste can be seen in hymns whose melodies are directly inspired by popular tunes heard on radio and television, the words of which have been composed by mediocre lyric writers; it can be seen in the way in which the choirs of certain churches are organized; the way that sanctuaries are cluttered with incomplete sets of old-looking furniture made without the least attempt at elegance or refinement and arranged without the least concern for harmony; altars and altar linens of

---

[36] Cf. nos. 292–93 (2000 edition).
[37] No. 294.

a sometimes dubious cleanliness; the addition of placards and banners that have no more than sentimental value; the use of photocopied sheets or disposable Mass booklets in place of the altar Missal for the celebration of the Eucharist, even though the Pope has asked for "liturgical books to be published in a form, at long last, that can be regarded as established on a long-term basis and presented in a way that is worthy of the mysteries that are being celebrated".[38]

Bad taste manifests itself as well in the way the liturgical actors behave and move, in the gap that is often noticeable between the ritual gesture to be performed and the words that accompany it, and in the way in which elements that are not in harmony with one another are jumbled together: in a certain baroque church, for example, the celebrant uses a simple earthen vase as a chalice. Elsewhere, you have a bishop who wears an eighteenth-century mitre, even while being dressed in a sort of loosely flowing, shapeless alb and wearing a garish colored stole, which on the face of it looks cheap and worthless.

The pastor of an important parish in Paris pointed out this lack of consistency and coherence observable with a good number of celebrants: he had assisted, he wrote in a newspaper column, at a Corpus Christi Mass during which the priest had used a splendid monstrance for the procession, even though, a few minutes earlier, Communion had been distributed in wicker baskets that the faithful passed along to each other.

Finally, bad taste appears in certain false attitudes (what

---

[38] John Paul II, apostolic letter *Vicesimus quintus annus*, no. 20.

is to be thought of celebrants who put on suave, honeyed voices to address the congregation?) and in the habit adopted of no longer wearing the prescribed liturgical vestments. In fact, there are many who, in order to preside over the Eucharist, are content to put on one of those modern sorts of albs whose fluttering looseness, by stressing flaws of dress and body instead of toning them down and improving them, only draws attention to the individualism of the person instead of highlighting his ministry in the Church.[39]

Is it not high time people reviewed the bad habits that have been adopted, which, in becoming widespread, have led to making worship insipid and to fostering division among the faithful?

It would be prudent to keep watch over the elements of liturgical worship, making sure they remain in perfect agreement and mutual harmony. In fact, is not the high incidence today of bad taste something that points to an absence of serious theological formation, which, when coupled with the errors of modern education, engenders a weakening of the sense of the sacred in general and liturgical sensibilities in particular?

The need to search for some aspect of beauty in liturgical celebrations remains essential: intimately linked as it is to the sense of the sacred, the beautiful allows the elimination from liturgical worship of all the rather dubious and sometimes even degrading and depraved ele-

---

[39] Cf. John Paul II, letter *Dominicae cenae* to all the bishops of the Church on the Mystery and Worship of the Eucharist (February 24, 1980), no. 12.

ments that stem from certain features of our present-day "anti-culture".

To recover the plastic beauty of gesture, vestments, and other objects is also to allow the liturgy to remain buffered from all the strange elements that are foreign to worship, not to mention all the human components that often aim only at facilitating a projection of the self, with all the ambiguities that are apt to be associated with this turn of events.

No celebration can do without a search for and expression of the beauty that is integral to its makeup, for the liturgy is indeed—as Dom Guéranger emphasized in the nineteenth century—the "divine aesthetic of our faith".[40]

Thus today the aesthetics of divine worship should once again become the constant concern of pastors, inasmuch as it is a reflection of the faith of the celebrating community for which they are responsible. As is noted once again by the restorer of Benedictine life in France, it is the faith that has been the guiding principle of all the splendid wonders of Christian aesthetics.[41]

Has it perhaps been forgotten that the constitution *Sacrosanctum concilium* lays a great deal of stress on the necessary beauty of every liturgical action? The liturgy, it is made clear in the text of the Council, should be performed with "dignity",[42], in a "correct and orderly manner"[43], on "well-planned" altars that have a "noble

---

[40] Prosper Guéranger, *Institutions liturgiques*, 2d ed. (Paris and Brussels: Société Génerale de Librairie Catholique, 1878–1885), 2:87.

[41] Ibid., 3:341.

[42] SC 28 and 80.

[43] SC 29.

shape''.[44] The rites themselves should be distinguished by a "noble simplicity"[45]; whatever is used in the service of worship should avoid "distortion of forms, lack of artistic worth, mediocrity, or pretense", all of which run the risk of promoting a faulty sense of devotion.[46]

How is a beautiful liturgy to be achieved? Are particular gifts and talents necessary in the attainment of this end? Is the aesthetics of worship the privileged domain of certain parishes that have extraordinary means at their disposal? Every member of the faithful who is given the responsibility of organizing a celebration ought always to remember that it is first and foremost the Church herself who gives us the liturgy. Thus it is the Church who provides us with our texts and hymns, which shows us the gestures to be made and the attitudes to be adopted. So if we celebrate the Eucharist by wanting to do what the Church tells us to do and in the manner in which the Church tells us to do it, then everything will be good and beautiful.

As for the officiating priest, his role consists not so much in adding the aesthetic dimension as in highlighting the *sacrum* contained in the Eucharist. The *sacrum*—what we mean by this is the holy, sacred character that the liturgical action possesses in itself—should not be confused with a sacralization of worship, that is to say, something that comes from the outside and is added to

---

[44] SC 128.
[45] SC 34.
[46] SC 124–25.

the Mass *to make it beautiful* or *to make it appealing to people*.

The *sacrum*, from which true beauty of worship emanates, is already to be found in the liturgy, insofar as the liturgy plunges its roots into the soil of the Last Supper on Holy Thursday, which was the founding rite of our celebrations. Thus it is in the action performed by Christ that we find the foundations of our liturgy, and, by way of consequence, it is from this action that emanates the only true beauty that each member of the faithful has a right to find in every celebration of the eucharist.[47]

Only the respectful piety of the celebrant accomplishing a task that infinitely exceeds his human capacities can guarantee the aesthetics of the liturgy. For respectful piety —which we need to rediscover in our day and age—will always be superior to the talents of men and altogether beyond the know-how of the best of parish liturgical teams.

4. The "deprivatization" of the liturgy

In his letter for the twenty-fifth anniversary of the Council's Constitution on the Sacred Liturgy, Pope John Paul II cites the "privatization of the religious sphere" coupled with "a rejection of institutions as such" as being two of the elements that have made the liturgical restoration desired by Vatican II so difficult.

It is true that, in the wake of the Council, numerous members of the faithful—both clergy and laity— attempted to make the liturgy a purely personal affair: such being the case, the celebration of Mass became some-

---

[47] John Paul II, *Vicesimus quintus annus*, no. 11.

thing of a playground for private experiments, and this led to horrific abuses.

In point of fact, the members of the faithful privatize the liturgy inasmuch as they no longer know—much less understand—that liturgical rites are not to be reinvented from day to day on the basis of changing situations or feelings or subjective principles, but that they proceed from an objective reality that is received from the Church and exists independently of those who participate in it.

From time out of mind, one of the risks the liturgy has run is having itself *trapped* or *co-opted* by the individualistic spirit in man; but since the beginning of the twentieth century, this danger has intensified, and this is in large part due to the pressure exerted by a modern mentality that is a direct heir to the philosophy of the Enlightenment.

It is forbidden to forbid. This was the cry in May 1968. Modern man believed he could attain happiness by freeing his personality and liberating himself from the shackles of established laws and rules. In reality, he only rendered himself ever more isolated in a kind of cult of the self-satisfied "me"; more or less pronounced expressions of this "me" can be found in certain present-day communities that have an excessive tendency at times to celebrate themselves through liturgies that they invent from scratch and fabricate to their own specifications.

Now the Church has always wanted her liturgy to be able to escape this dangerously narrow state of confinement. This is the reason why she has given rules to be followed that apply to everyone, from the Pope on down to the least of the faithful. These rules subject the individual to a norm that is all the more liberating because it is higher than he is, since its essence is divine.

In every celebration, therefore, the Church assigns a role and a station to each person and keeps a watchful eye on the good order of things. In the end, this sort of discipline is the only way to take true care of the person, to respect his rights, and to offer him some measure of protection and defense. Thus each individual has a unique and indispensable place that he alone can and should occupy, and in this way he plays a role that works toward the harmony of the celebration.

It is this principle that meshes perfectly with the text of the Council where it declares that "in liturgical celebrations, whether as a minister or as one of the faithful, each person should perform his role by doing solely and totally what the nature of things and liturgical norms require of him." [48]

Thus the liturgy should obey objective norms, so that through it each person may manage his own freedom and give a meaning to the activities of his personal life, without at the same time changing the quality of the official, public prayer to which all the faithful have a right.

Contrary to what has often been reiterated these past few years, the liturgical norms fixed by the Church do not make for rigid, ossified celebrations: on the contrary, observing the laws that govern celebration allows the integrity of divine worship to be protected and pride of place to be reserved for the movements of men's hearts

---

[48] SC 28.

in their most mysterious, most intimate, and deepest aspects.

It is only when the liturgy obeys objective norms and evades the manipulations of the celebrant or some group or other[49] that it possesses to a unique degree the art of giving expression to the most secret and most genuine states of our soul. Often it is because the faithful feel these things in an entirely natural way that they sometimes prefer to leave parishes where liturgies more or less outside the norms are celebrated and that, come Sunday, they make their way to monasteries or, failing that, to chapels looked after by traditionalist groups or Lefebvrite communities. But whatever the case, these are places where they know the rites will be respected.

Dom Odo Casel taught that

> Catholic worship shows highly objective traits. On these traits it leaves the imprint of its *shape and form*. Its character does not come from subjective whims or a gush of personal sentiment, passing emotions, or the effects wrought by voices that are inflamed by passion; it is a result of objective clarity, of transpersonal content rooted in the divine and eternal. This objective content seeks and finds its expression quite naturally in forms that are reserved, tranquil, moderate, and capable of tempering an exuberance of ideas and feelings, of stylizing and spiritualizing that which is human.

The "privatization of religion" always leads eventually to the celebration of Masses where people take less account of the rites established by the Church precisely to

---

[49] Cf. Bishop Lagrange, in *Enquête sur la messe traditionnelle*.

the degree they seek to personalize the liturgy in order to humanize it and make it more accessible, or so they think.

From a purely sociological point of view, this way of doing things may seem effective. But from an ecclesiological, theological point of view, it must indeed be acknowledged that it leads to failure; practiced to excess these last thirty years, it has emptied churches and at the same time divided Catholics. If, in the midst of all this, any of these Catholics were attentive to what was happening, they quickly realized that Masses composed on the basis of this neo-ritual approach could only end in the liberation of the most childish and immature elements in human psychology.

At this point, it is useful to recall the warning issued by Pope John Paul II in a letter addressed to the bishops of the Church:[50]

> Every priest who offers the Holy Sacrifice should recall that during this Sacrifice it is not only he with his community that is praying but the whole Church, which is thus expressing in this Sacrament her spiritual unity, among other ways by the use of the approved liturgical text. To call this position ''mere insistence on uniformity'' would only show ignorance of the objective requirements of authentic unity, and would be a symptom of harmful individualism.

And John Paul II goes on to add:

> This subordination of the minister, of the celebrant, to that Mysterium which has been entrusted to him by the

---

[50] *Dominicae cenae*, no. 12.

Church for the good of the whole People of God, should also find expression in the observance of the liturgical requirements concerning the celebration of the Holy Sacrifice. These refer for example to dress, and in particular to the vestments worn by the celebrant. . . . In normal conditions to ignore the liturgical directives can be interpreted as a lack of respect towards the Eucharist, dictated perhaps by individualism or by an absence of a critical sense concerning current opinions, or by a certain lack of a spirit of faith.

Therefore, if we go by the teachings of the Pope, the person who privatizes the liturgy in order to give it a more personal "coloring" risks appearing, to the eyes of the faithful, as someone whose spirit of faith is lacking. This, it should be said, is a serious cloud of suspicion for a person to be under!

The words of John Paul II are echoed by the *Directory for the Ministry and Life of Permanent Deacons*: it makes it clear in fact that "manipulation of the liturgy is tantamount to depriving it of the riches of the mystery of Christ, whom it contains, and may well signify presumption toward what has been established by the Church's wisdom." [51]

Would not a true and genuine *deprivatization* of the liturgy be an effective means of reestablishing unity around the Roman Missal? In any case, such a turn of events would be in response to a legitimate desire on the part of the faithful, who want not just dignified celebrations but also celebrations from which the *patchwork elements* have

---

[51] Cf. *Directory*, no. 30.

been eliminated: by the all too human aspects they inevitably display,[52] the meddlesome interventions undertaken by those who are actors in the liturgy pollute the rites of the Church, ruin the tranquil progress of the liturgy, and in the end always erect a screen between God, who is present on the altar, and the men and women who have come to encounter him.[53]

---

[52] "The human place occupied by the priest assumes too much importance. . . . Not to mention the stream of men, women, and young people who march up to the microphone to recount their stories and give their witness. I also believe that, by celebrating in this way, the human aspect of the principal celebrant, no less than that of the laymen who are constantly intervening, forms a screen between the member of the faithful and God. Now who is the mediator between God and man? It is Christ. Individuals have taken his place. . . . There really is too much in the way of commentary and chatter. . . . Under the pretext of having a communitarian liturgy, the faithful are enlisted in the effort: they have to 'build community', they have to shake hands with one another, they have to kiss and hug one another, they have to raise their arms. . . . I believe that the interior dimension is of absolutely capital importance in the Catholic liturgy. The way in which activities marked by togetherness are encouraged and favored by force of commentary is not something I care for personally. It has been said, and it is not entirely untrue, that things have gotten a little bit too much like Protestant worship" (Father Michel Lelong, *Reconstruire la liturgie* [Paris: Guibert, 1997]).

[53] Cf. John Paul II, *Dominicae cenae.*

CHAPTER TEN

Conclusion

Forty years after the close of Vatican II, the implementation of the liturgy that was desired by the Church still poses many questions and raises significant problems. It must indeed be admitted that the incompetence of some combined with the silence of others has created a situation in which the constitution *Sacrosanctum concilium* has remained a dead letter: the People of God have found that the liturgy to which they have a right has been betrayed or falsified.

In a majority of parishes, the clergy, surrounded by laymen who are themselves more or less clericalized,[1] are still making up liturgies in which attitudes, gestures, hymns, and prayers that are not those of the Roman Missal are

---

[1] "In my parish, the liturgy is in a sorry state. As this bad liturgy is produced by some very decent people, I dare not utter a word of protest because I am afraid of upsetting them, they are so full of goodwill. . . . They are quite nice, you know. But I find their liturgy appallingly dull and insipid. In fact, this impoverishment of the liturgy was not something that the faithful wanted. They were never really consulted. Furthermore, more than 50 percent of Christians no longer practice their faith. The changes have been made by a minority of the clergy" (Jacques Dupâquier, in Michel Lelong, *Reconstruire la liturgie* [Paris: Guibert, 1997]).

being imposed. But these bad habits are entrenched and no longer seem to bother many people.

Forty years after the Council, there are still pastors to be found who admit that they have never read either the whole of the constitution *Sacrosanctum concilium* or the *General Instruction of the Roman Missal*. It is clear that some bishops are not acquainted with the rites of the present-day liturgy and still do not know what they have to do during eucharistic celebrations; given these conditions, how could they seem to believers to be caretakers of the liturgy?

There are still celebrants to be found who, displaying an authoritarianism that a person would have thought belonged to the past, still systematically refuse to give their permission when the faithful request Gregorian chant or the celebration of a Latin Mass (using the current *Ordo*).[2]

The situation will continue to get worse as long as the professors and seminarians in houses of formation for future clergy are not obliged to know and respect the current Missal in all its fullness, first in its Latin form, which is its basis, and then in its vernacular form, which is only a potential outgrowth from it.[3]

----

[2] Canon 214: "The Christian faithful have the right to worship God according to the prescriptions of their own rite approved by the legitimate pastors of the Church"; canon 928: "The Eucharist is to be celebrated in the Latin language or in another language provided the liturgical texts have been legitimately approved." From *The Code of Canon Law*, trans. under the auspices of the Canon Law Society of America (Washington, D.C.: Canon Law Society of America, 1983).

[3] For the moment, as far as we know, the full liturgical formation desired by the Second Vatican Council exists in only one place [in France]: this is the Communauté Saint-Martin (53, rue du Château,

These days everybody concedes that the principal reason why the traditionalist movement was able to spread and call for a return to old forms of the liturgy is that members of the faithful had prepared the ground for it by favoring progressive liturgical trends—to varying degrees—in virtually every parish. How did this progressive trend manifest itself? In the first place, "altars facing the people" were systematically erected in places where there was no reason for them to be. Inevitably this led to a destabilization of liturgical space, an impoverishment of liturgical ceremony, and a change in clerical patterns of behavior. Then altar-boy groups were abolished,[4] and the use of Latin and Gregorian chant was forbidden.[5] All of this led to numerous parish choirs being disbanded, even though they had been doing their part to enhance the rites of worship. Congregations were silenced, or else the faithful were forced to quit singing anything except for brief worthless refrains. Either that or they were made to sing repetitive hymns that were utterly out of place be-

---

41120 Candé s/Beuvron). It is good to know that in the dioceses that have received priests coming from this Community, liturgical life in parishes has quickly blossomed anew, to the great joy of both the faithful and the bishops.

[4] Or else girls were brought into the ranks in order slowly to get rid of the boys (which has led to a decreased use of the rites of incensing, preparation of the altar, the offertory, and the entrance and closing processions, and so on).

[5] "The Bishops . . . are conscious that the inherited treasure of sacred music as constituted by Gregorian chant and polyphony must be maintained, for when these are used judiciously, they enhance prayer and the participation of the faithful. . . . Latin hymns still have their value" (*Directive des évêques de France sur la musique sacrée* [Directive of the bishops of France on sacred music], May 6, 1964).

fore the beginning of Mass. In addition to all this, lay-men, true to a certain social and psychological type,[6] were brought on the scene to play roles that irritated the faith-ful.[7]

Lastly, there has been an abandonment of the prescribed liturgical vestments. This has led to a trivialization of worship and to greater importance being attributed to the personality of the celebrant[8] than to his ministerial function. In turn, there has been an increase in explanations and commentaries, which pollute the liturgy.[9]

------

[6] With a somewhat realistic sense of humor, young priests call these "committed lay people" "wannabe priests". The phrase is an apt and expressive description of the situation.

[7] In rural areas, where parish life often intertwines with local political life, it is not unusual to note that, in the time leading up to an election, those of the faithful who aspire to a post as mayor or town councillor offer their services as liturgical animators; it is a way of raising one's profile with the portion of the electorate who practice their faith. But once the elections are over, the liturgical animator is no more to be seen.

[8] Cardinal Ratzinger notes that, in the sixteenth century, Luther replaced the cassock with an academic gown in order to demonstrate clearly that, from that point on, it would be the learned exegete and no longer the ordained priest who would be called on to be the real decision-maker in the Church. Similarly, at the present time, the abandonment of ecclesiastical dress followed by the abandonment of liturgical vestments has been the sign, as it were, of a progressive laicization of the clergy, a prelude to the invasion of sanctuaries by lay people who want to show that from now on it will be the "rank and file member of the faithful" and no longer the Magisterium of the Church that is to be called on to be the real decision-maker in matters liturgical. (Cf. J. Ratzinger, *Milestones: Memoirs 1927–1977*, trans. Erasmo Leiva-Merikakis [San Francisco: Ignatius Press, 1998], 133–34).

[9] "A long-winded, garrulous liturgy risks becoming a tool, which is to say that it comes to be used for ends other than itself. . . . Thus the

Whether one wants to acknowledge the fact or not, current liturgical practices are the fruit of an errant aimlessness that is all too longstanding and that has led to the creation of two large, opposing classes of the faithful.

The first class includes those for whom the liturgy has become an occasion for self-assertion through their appropriation of the rites, arranging them, if necessary, according to the tastes and needs of the moment. The second category includes those for whom the liturgy must lead to self-effacement, in order not to hinder the action of the Holy Spirit.

Thus in parishes we find, on the one hand, partisans of an active liturgy in which each person is called to participate in a kind of collective show and, on the other hand, partisans of a more contemplative liturgy in which each person is called to recollection and meditation. In the first case, people seek to invent rites that are meant to correspond to the activity they want to pursue during the celebration, while, in the second case, people seek to internalize the rites they have received from the Church. There is no doubt but that unity will be hard to achieve.

---

liturgy is neither a time nor a place that is adaptable to catechesis. . . . The distinctive feature of the liturgy involves giving precedence to experience. Things are first experienced, and only afterward are they reflected on, analyzed, and explained. 'To celebrate first and then to understand': this is an adage that some may find strange, or else they may see it as an instance of anti-intellectual obscurantism. . . . The Fathers of the Church held it on principle that mystagogical catechesis, that is to say, a detailed explanation of the sacred mysteries, came only after the sacraments of initiation. . . . Their pedagogical approach was based on the senses: first you participate and experience, and only after that do you explain" (Cardinal Danneels, in Lelong, *Reconstruire*).

The Council, however, does not underestimate these two tendencies: action and contemplation belong to the very nature of the Church and thus to the deepest nature of the men and women who make up the Mystical Body of Christ. But, so that there may be harmony and equilibrium, *Sacrosanctum concilium* recalls that in the Church "the human is directed and subordinated to the divine, the visible likewise to the invisible, action to contemplation, and this present world to that city yet to come, which we seek."[10]

It ought to be the same in the liturgy, which should proclaim the mystery of our salvation, show the living Church, and edify the believer by bolstering his energies instead of exhausting them in a sterile activism. Therefore pastors—in union with all the faithful—who want the liturgy to be restored to its role of being a leaven of Christian unity ought to work with a view to giving back to the Roman Missal—and to it alone—all the authority it had before the Second Vatican Council. They must firmly and definitively stop treating the liturgy like a reality with variable contours that are contingent on time, place, personal tastes, and sociological conditions.[11]

But how many Christians are prepared to carry out such a program, which goes against the grain of all the liturgical practices that have been in place at this point for decades in entire dioceses by virtue of a false interpretation of Vatican II's constitution *Sacrosanctum concilium* and

---

[10] SC 2.

[11] Cf. Bishop Bernard Dupire, address to the International Symposium on the Liturgy at the Abbey of Solesmes, *Actes du Colloque* (Rosheim, Association APL).

in defiance of the elementary rights held by each member of the faithful?

If a solution leading to the recovery of the Roman Rite is not to be found in the ongoing liturgical anarchy of the present day, neither is it to be found in the coexistence of two forms of one and the same Roman Rite, the old and the new, or in the production of a new *Ordo missae*: when it comes to the liturgy, compromise is never a solution.

The solution of the future lies in the manner in which the faithful, both clergy and laity, are to be invited to treat the liturgy; for it is no longer the difference between two missals or between two forms of the Roman Rite that is the most important factor today, but the traditional or anti-traditional way of approaching the celebration of the Eucharist.[12]

All people of goodwill who currently participate in the development and planning of parish liturgies should relearn what the liturgy really is: it is not a matter of fashioning beautiful Masses, as you would put on a beautiful show or as you would stage a beautiful event. It is a matter of implementing accurately the rites and symbols in the Roman Missal, by attending to their quality and truthfulness, so that each member of the faithful who makes the effort to appropriate them can enter into the depths of the mystery of faith, which is offered to everyone by the celebrating Church.[13]

---

[12] Cardinal Ratzinger, lecture given on September 25, 1995, at the Abbaye du Barroux.

[13] Cf. Joseph Vandrisse, in *Famille chrétienne*, 1086 (November 5, 1998): 11.

Thus it is urgent to recover the traditional way of celebrating Mass according to the current Missal. The liturgy from before Vatican II can help us a great deal: not by serving as a refuge, as is all too often the case nowadays when it has become unhappily necessary to escape the disobedience of certain members of the clergy or the incompetence of all too many teams of liturgical animators, but by serving as a point of reference in the long history of the Roman liturgy.

Using this as a basis, the faithful, aided by their pastors, will be able to revive the genuine legacy of the Second Vatican Council, a legacy that is not what people are apt to see at present being put into practice in a majority of parishes.

> Goodwill does not make for good liturgy any more than good feelings make for good literature. All priests and liturgical animators should have a solid knowledge of the teaching of the Council and of the content of the introductions to the rituals. Since the sacraments are signs from God and an undertaking of the Church, honesty demands that we know what sign God is producing for us through Christ and what undertaking the Church is anxious to accomplish. The creativity that is desirable in the liturgy does not lie in whim: it lies in the intelligent application of the norms.[14]

While it is legitimate to come to Mass with all our human components, as excellent or weak as they may be, it is perilous to want celebrations fashioned in the image of our desires, whether they be progressive or traditionalist

---

[14] Bishop F. Favreau, *La Liturgie* (Paris: Desclée, 1983).

in nature. Only the liturgy celebrated as the Church requires it to be celebrated can be the matrix of what we are called to become as Christians: starting with a renewal of "liturgical awareness",[15] it is urgent for us to relearn how to respect and celebrate the liturgy in all its splendor, both in cathedrals and in rural churches and monasteries, so that it may once again become that "springboard to the divine" that men who are seeking genuine spiritual values need so badly.

---

[15] Ratzinger, *Milestones*, 148.

Appendix

On October 26, 1998, Pope John Paul II addressed a message to members of the faithful attached to the rites of the preconciliar Roman liturgy, who had come to Rome on the occasion of the tenth anniversary of the motu proprio *Ecclesia Dei adflicta.*

The Sovereign Pontiff clearly specified how the motu proprio should be understood and what significance should be attributed to tradition:

> I offer my cordial greetings to you, dear pilgrims who have wished to come to Rome for the 10th anniversary of the Motu Proprio *Ecclesia Dei*, to strengthen and renew your faith in Christ and your fidelity to the Church. Dear friends, your presence with the "Successor of Peter who has the chief responsibility for watching over the unity of the Church" (First Vatican Ecumenical Council, First Dogmatic Constitution *Pastor aeternus*) is especially significant.
>
> In order to safeguard the treasure which Jesus has entrusted to her, and resolutely turned towards the future, it is the Church's duty to reflect constantly on her link with the Tradition that comes to us from the Lord through the Apostles, as it has been built up throughout history. According to the spirit of conversion in the Apostolic Letter *Tertio millennio adveniente* (nn. 14, 32, 34, 50), I urge all Catholics to perform acts of unity and to renew their loyalty to the Church, so that their legitimate diversity and different sensitivities, which deserve respect, will not di-

vide them but spur them to proclaim the Gospel together; thus, moved by the Spirit who makes all charisms work towards unity, they can all glorify the Lord, and salvation will be proclaimed to all nations.

I hope all the members of the Church will remain heirs to the faith received from the Apostles, worthily and faithfully celebrated in the holy mysteries with fervour and beauty, in order to receive grace ever more abundantly (cf. Ecumenical Council of Trent, session VII, 3 March 1547, Decree on the Sacraments) and to live in a deep and intimate relationship with the divine Trinity. While confirming the well-founded good of the liturgical reform desired by the Second Vatican Council and carried out by Pope Paul VI, the Church also shows her understanding for people "who feel attached to some previous liturgical and disciplinary forms" (Motu Proprio *Ecclesia Dei*, n. 5) The Motu Proprio *Ecclesia Dei* must be interpreted and applied in this perspective; I hope that it will all be lived in the spirit of the Second Vatican Council, in full harmony with Tradition, aiming at unity in charity and fidelity to the Truth.

It is on account of the "Holy Spirit's activity, by which the whole flock of Christ is maintained in the unity of faith and makes progress in it" (Dogmatic Constitution *Lumen Gentium*, n. 25), that the Successor of Peter and the Bishops, Successors of the Apostles, teach the Christian mystery; in a quite particular way, gathered in Ecumenical Councils *cum Petro* and *sub Petro*, they confirm and affirm the doctrine of the Church, the faithful heir to the Tradition now in existence for almost 20 centuries as a living reality that progresses, giving new energy to the ecclesial community as a whole. The most recent Ecumenical Councils—Trent, Vatican I, Vatican II—were particularly committed to explaining the mystery of faith and undertook the necessary reforms for the Church's good, while being concerned for continuity with the apostolic Tradition, already noted by St Hippolytus.

Therefore it is primarily the task of the Bishops, in communion with the Successor of Peter, to lead the flock with firmness and charity so that the Catholic faith is safeguarded everywhere (cf. Paul VI, Apostolic Exhortation *Quinque iam anni; Code of Canon Law*, can. 386) and celebrated with dignity. In fact, according to the formula of St Ignatius of Antioch, "where the Bishop is, there is the Church as well" (*Letter to the Smyrneans*, VIII, 2). I therefore extend a fraternal invitation to Bishops to show understanding and renewed pastoral attention to the faithful who are attached to the former rite and, on the threshold of the third millennium, to help all Catholics live the celebration of the holy mysteries with a devotion that truly nourishes their spiritual life and is a source of peace.

Dear brothers and sisters, as I entrust you to the intercession of the Virgin Mary, perfect model of the *sequela Christi* and Mother of the Church, I impart my Apostolic Blessing to you and to all your loved ones.[1]

---

[1] John Paul II, "Legitimate Diversity Must Not Divide", no. 5, *L'Osservatore romano* 45 (November 11, 1998): 7.